AF491415

52-Week Women's Retirement Devotional: Awaken to Your Identity, Flourish in God's Love, Strengthen Your Purpose & Rediscover a Joyful, Radiant Life

ISBN: 979-8-9921551-2-9

God's Perfect Timing: A 21-Day Bible Study & Daily Devotional Through the Book of Ruth

The 90-Day Self-Forgiveness Journal for Christian Women: Daily Scripture, Prayer & Guided Journaling to Release Hurts, Find Peace, & Walk in God's Freedom

For all of the Grandmas in my life, who had lovely purple hair, glowing like angels, for the pretty pins they wore on their dresses, and for holding me close as a child as they whispered, 'Everything is going to be OK."

Thank you Grandma Watkins, Grandma Wren, and Nellie Wayre – who was never really my grandmother, but loved me like one.

Introduction

> *"The righteous will flourish like a palm tree and grow like a cedar in Lebanon. Planted in the house of the LORD, they will flourish in the courts of our God. In old age they will still bear fruit; healthy and green they will remain."*
> Psalm 92:12–14

Welcome to Your Next Chapter

Retirement arrives with freedom, but it also brings questions that no financial planner or operating manual ever seems to answer. Can you really call these years the best years of your life? You may have so many questions, like these:

Who Are You Now?

How can I manage my days when the structure of a work routine disappears?

What About This Isolated Feeling?

If I'm single, how do I manage being alone all day? If I'm married, how do we spend the whole day together?

Will I Be Worried About Money All the Time?

What do I do when the numbers on the statement begin to shrink?

How Can I Be Useful Without Stress?

Will I become the target of every volunteer committee?

How Can I Feel Fully Alive When My Body is Falling Apart?

How can I still make these the best years of my life?

God is not surprised by your questions.

In fact, God has already anticipated everything and has answered them in some of the most beautiful passages in the Bible. His version of retirement and aging is one of flourishing, vibrancy, and growth; yes, even despite our very real physical limitations.

God sees you in retirement in a special way. You are His intentional handiwork, fearfully and wonderfully made, known and called by name long before you ever held a job title.

He doesn't see you as fading or finished, but as flourishing and evergreen—a woman wearing her years as a crown of glory, inwardly renewed day by day.

He sees you as radiant and completely unashamed, equipped with a spirit of power, love, and self-discipline rather than timidity.

You are more than a conqueror, as bold as a lion, and fiercely sustained by the One who promises to carry you.

In His eyes, your path is not dimming into the twilight; it is soaring on eagle's wings, shining ever brighter into the full light of day, ready for the good works He prepared in advance just for you.

This book shows you that God isn't surprised by any of your questions. He has already accounted for them.

If you want a preview of the promises God has already written for you, jump to the back of this book to see a list of 17 "Flourish Scriptures."

Claim Your Free Gift

Over the next year, you will move through four stages that reflect the natural rhythm of spiritual growth: **Awaken** – rediscovering your identity in Christ beyond roles or titles. **Flourish** – learning to receive God's daily grace and restoration. **Strengthen** – building spiritual endurance and trusting God with the future. **Fruitful** – using the wisdom of your life to bless others and leave a legacy of faith.

To get started on your Flourish journey, download your free Bonus Content, your Flourish Journey Map. This download includes weekly cards with scripture anchors, and weekly activities for each of the Four Phases. The final phase includes a page to write your Flourish Manifesto. You can access your free gift through the QR code.

Phase One: Awaken – Weeks 1-13

Ephesians 2:10 · Jeremiah 1:5 · Isaiah 43:1

The alarm goes off for the last time. The retirement party never helped you answer that one lingering question: "Who am I now?" Phase One is about sitting with that question long enough to let God answer it. Over the next thirteen weeks, you will begin to peel back the layers of title, productivity, and professional identity to find something far more solid underneath. Before you started your career, you were already known — loved before you produced a single thing the world calls valuable, and called by a name that belongs only to you. The good works God prepared for you in advance have not gone anywhere.

Week 1: The Last Day

For we are God's workmanship, created in Christ Jesus to do good works, which God prepared in advance as our way of life. Ephesians 2:10

There is a surreal moment — maybe you've already lived it, maybe it's coming — when the career chapter finally closes. The badge is turned in. Someone else will sit in your chair by Monday. And somewhere in the back of your mind, a small voice whispers: Have I done the right thing?

Some women cry when they close the laptop for the last time, and some feel like dancing. Most finally turn off the alarm clock for a good sleep-in.

The congratulatory words are kind, and the smile you're wearing is real. But underneath there is an unsettling feeling that isn't grief exactly, but carries grief's weight. It's more like a fleeting, drifting feeling that you don't yet have a word for. But it's definitely trying to tell you something. You might have been anticipating retirement for years or months, because this is what you wanted. But now that it's here, the whole retirement thing feels stranger than you expected.

What you do need to watch for in the coming weeks is the emptiness that can sneak in without warning — the idea that your purpose went out the door with the title. That belief alone can cause you to fill your time with meaningless activities or overschedule your days with appointments and commitments that leave you feeling drained rather than fulfilled.

Scripture offers the comfort that the door you're walking through is not the end, but a continuation of the life God has been creating for you all this time. Ephesians 2:10 says nothing about career, title, or productivity. It says you are His "workmanship." In the original Greek, Paul uses the word poiema, which means poem, or divine craftsmanship. Some translations call it handiwork, or workmanship, but the root is the same: you are a masterpiece. You were made with love for things that go beyond any label, title, or position you've held. And the good works God prepared in advance for you haven't gone anywhere just because your career has ended.

So give yourself this first week to feel what you feel without rushing to fix it. You don't need a plan by Friday. You don't need to be thriving yet. You just need to show up, pay attention, and trust that the One who prepared good works for you in advance knew exactly what He was doing when He designed this particular, ordinary morning.

Each week, you'll find scripture, journal prompts, activities, and prayers to help you stay attuned to what sparks joy in you. And that joy, it turns out, aligns perfectly with how God created you and how He loves you.

"Retire to something, not just from something. Having a plan is the difference between living a full, busy life and letting the years pass you by." —
Stephanie M.

This Week's Activity

This week we will get started with the Morning Radiance Practice. Buy a pen that you actually love to write with and a journal. The physical pleasure of a good pen on a real page

is part of what helps make this practice enjoyable, and a habit that you look forward to.

Before you protest and say, "journaling is not for me," consider the numerous long-term brain health benefits of journaling. Research from Rush University Medical Center found that consistently engaging in mentally stimulating activities like writing can lower the risk of developing Alzheimer's disease by nearly 40%.

More importantly, there are profound faith-building benefits to journaling. Some of the greatest writers, preachers, and leaders in church history, from St. Augustine to Oswald Chambers to Ann Voskamp, have made journaling part of their daily practice.

If you still think it sounds like too much, try journaling for at least 21 days.

Something powerful happens in your brain when you write by hand rather than typing. A study from the Norwegian University of Science and Technology found that handwriting creates far more elaborate brain connectivity patterns than typing on a keyboard, activating sensory and motor systems essential for memory formation and learning.

But the most important reason to journal is that there is a profound cathartic release when you pour out your thoughts in a letter no one will ever see. By page two, something starts to release in your heart and your brain; you've cleared the fog, and suddenly an answer to a problem you haven't been able to solve for years pops into your mind.

For these benefits, I call this the Morning Radiance Practice,

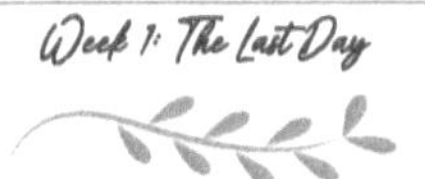

because journaling can help you transform from the inside out.

It is rooted in this promise:

> *"Because of the loving devotion of the LORD we are not consumed, for His mercies never fail. They are new every morning; great is Your faithfulness!" Lamentations 3:22–23*

Dew arrives in the night. It is already there when you open your eyes. It is not something you produce or earn. You don't generate the dew.

You take an active step to go out and collect what God has created for you. In the same way, God's renewal arrives quietly each morning. You show up with pen to paper, clearing away the cobwebs so you can see the amazing work God is already doing, and what His will is for you today.

Some mornings, you may feel like you have nothing to write. Do the exercise anyway. Even if you fill the pages by repeating the line:

I think this is pointless!

Write faithfully for two pages. Write about your fears and your sadness; pour out an angry letter of things you just need to get off your chest. You might also try writing your honest, heartfelt prayers as letters rather than silently thinking them. Tie your prayers to a scripture and write them out in full.

Important: If questions come up, circle them, or mark them in some way; you'll need them at night at bedtime.

By page three, something almost always shifts. New insights begin to surface. Problems you had forgotten about suddenly reveal solutions. Gratitude begins to replace frustration. And often, genuine praise to God appears on the page.

Journaling is a gift you can give yourself every morning to bring you clarity, peace, and a renewed perspective.

Optional Radiance Journal Prompts

- When you closed the "career" chapter of your life, what were your feelings underneath the smile?
- What role did you hold most tightly; don't limit it to your job title, but the way you thought of yourself in relation to your work? Who did you believe you were because of what you did?
- Ephesians 2:10 says you were created for good works prepared in advance. What is one you think might be waiting for you now?

Prayer

Lord, I didn't expect retirement to feel quite like this. I worked toward this day. Now that it's here, I'm not entirely sure who I am on this side of it. Remind me of the truth: that You made me with intention, that You've been writing this chapter for longer than I knew, and that the good works You prepared for me don't have a retirement date. Thank You that You are still writing the poem. In Jesus' name, Amen.

"...to put off your former way of life, your old self, which is being corrupted by its deceitful desires; to be renewed in the spirit of your minds; and to put on the new self, created to be like God in true righteousness and holiness."
Ephesians 4:22–24

Here comes the question everyone asks at the retirement party: So what are you going to do next?

It's meant to be encouraging and supportive. Standing there with a sheet cake that says "Congratulations," you might realize that a simple question can make you feel as if you suddenly have a brick sitting in your stomach. Because even if you do have a plan, it may feel shakier now that you're standing in it. But honestly, you didn't know that having a plan was a required prerequisite for well-wishers. You thought retirement meant relaxation, but the question "What are you going to do next?" seems to demand an itinerary.

The question itself is one worth unpacking. The calendar has always shown you what came next. Now the calendar is blank, and the doing is entirely up to you. That is either the most terrifying or the most exciting sentence you've read all week; possibly both.

While you worked, the clothes you chose defined your role. Maybe it was a blazer, scrubs, or special shoes. The clothes likely even shaped how you walked into a room; they told the world who you were.

And now the costume is optional. The closet is full of things that fit the old life, and you're standing in front of it on a

Wednesday morning, wondering what a woman like you wears when she isn't being that version of herself anymore.

Some women find the chance to change their look exhilarating. Others find it disorienting in a way they didn't anticipate. The identity you built over a career didn't develop overnight, and it won't be replaced overnight either. Give yourself the same grace you'd give a friend who just moved to a new city; she's not going to feel at home in the first week. That doesn't mean she made the wrong move.

This moment in front of the closet is more theological than it sounds. In Ephesians 4, is talking about the transition from an old identity to a new one. Put away the old self. Be renewed in the spirit of your mind. Put on the new. The old way of living, the old way of seeing yourself, the old patterns that were built around productivity and performance — those get set aside. In their place is something that fits who you are in Christ.

Notice that the renewal Paul describes in Ephesians 4 is ongoing. Present tense. Be renewed; not were renewed; not will eventually be renewed; renewed now. It's a continuous process, and that's actually good news.

So the closet is a good place to start. Not because what you wear is the point, but because the act of going through it is a physical practice that demands you to answer these questions: "What am I keeping because it still fits who I am?" and "What am I holding onto because letting go feels like admitting something has changed?"

Something has changed, and it's good. Let the closet be evidence of that.

This Week's Activity

Don't worry, while the Evening Radiance Practice echoes the Morning version, it takes far less time — and it's a practice that leads to peaceful, restful sleep, while training your mind to let go of the burdens of the day from your shoulders.

Plus, this evening practice builds on one of the most intimate ways that God speaks to us directly; and one we toss aside because we think it's too good to be true that God speaks to us while we sleep.

> *"For God speaks in one way and in another, yet no one notices. In a dream, in a vision in the night, when deep sleep falls upon men as they slumber on their beds, He opens their ears and terrifies them with warnings." Job 33:14–16*

The word terrifies here is an interesting one, but also comforting at the same time. God provides the "warning" to get our attention before it's too late. The question is, have you trained yourself to recognize Him in your dreams?

Right before you fall asleep, or at the end of the day, make a list of the questions, decisions, or problems that have you stuck (refer back to the questions from your morning writing session). Then ask God for His help to work on this list tonight while you "sleep on it." Releasing your burdens to God in this way is a powerful signal to your mind, allowing you to relax and get to sleep.

Like the morning practice, the process of writing it down allows you to see it on paper, so that you can let it go. God will answer. It might not be tomorrow, but His answer will become clear. Maybe even when you are doing your journaling tomorrow morning.

Another powerful entry to end your evening journaling is to write down three blessings from your day. This is an important way to overcome our brain's natural tendency to focus on the negative. This is why Scripture instructs us to do exactly this:

> *"Bless the LORD, O my soul, and do not forget all His kind deeds—" Psalm 103:2*

When we regularly count our blessings, we train our minds to recognize God's presence in everyday life. Soon, you will have trained your mind to recognize God's voice more clearly in your life, become more confident about your future, and see His blessings. You may discover that these practices become one of the most powerful habits of your retirement season.

Optional Radiance Journal Prompts

- When you think about your work wardrobe, does it feel like you? What did you like about the image it portrayed of you?
- Ephesians 4 describes renewal as an ongoing process rather than a one-time event. Where do you see that renewal already beginning in your life?
- If you had to describe who you are without referencing what you used to do, what would you say?

Lord, I've been wearing the same identity for a long time, and I didn't realize how much of it was built on what I produced rather than who I am. Help me set down what no longer fits. Help me stop reaching for the old costume out of habit, and show me what it looks like to put on the new self You've been preparing all along. The one that was always more You in me than me in a role. In Jesus' name, Amen.

Week 3: Known Before You Were Hired

> *"Before I formed you in the womb I knew you, and before you were born I set you apart." Jeremiah 1:5*

You work hard; you become known for your work; the work becomes part of how you introduce yourself at dinner parties and how you answer the question, "Tell me about yourself." The job starts to feel like a synonym for the self.

But there is a crucial difference between what you do, or did, and who you are. Most of us have let those two things blur together.

God knew you before any boss, client, or customer ever did. He knew you before your first performance review, your first promotion, before you knew which field you'd give your best years to. So, whether you made it to the corner office or spent your career in the same steady role, it makes no difference to God. He loved you before you even had the opportunity to produce a single thing the world would call valuable.

Your daily routine has changed, but God has been shaping you through the joyful seasons and the hard ones. And now that the calendar is a bit emptier, you get to become more fully yourself.

> *"After a few weeks, aside from missing a few coworkers, I was genuinely glad to be done with the career I had loved for many years. I didn't expect to feel that way so soon." — Patricia H.*

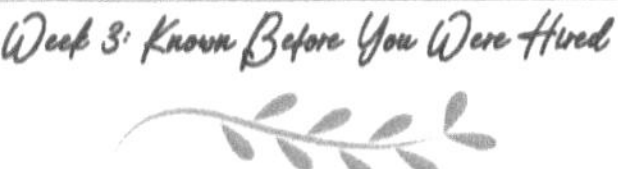

Read Jeremiah 1:5 slowly, then write your name in the blank: 'Before I formed ________ in the womb, I knew her.' Now write three things about yourself that were true long before your first job, your first title, or your first performance review.

Optional Radiance Journal Prompts

- How will you introduce yourself at parties? Will you say, I'm a retired ____________? Can you think of a way to say it without your job title?
- What do you know about yourself that has been consistently true long before your career began?
- Where did the line between your identity and your job blur most?
- If God set you apart before you were born, what do you think He had in mind about you that has nothing to do with the career you built?

Prayer

Lord, I think somewhere along the way I started to believe my role was the point of my identity. Help me find my way back to what You knew before any of that; before I had a resume, and that title. I want to live from that place now. Show me who I am. In Jesus' name, Amen.

"When you pass through the waters, I will be with you; and when you go through the rivers, they will not overwhelm you." Isaiah 43:2

For someone who has structured her days around productivity and the steady rhythm of a working life, the stillness can, after the newness wears off, feel less like rest and more like floating out to sea with nothing to hold onto.

That feeling has a name: adrift. Adrift and excited can happen at the same time. The same wide-open calendar that makes you feel untethered on Tuesday morning can feel like the greatest gift you've ever been given by Thursday afternoon.

Joshua knew something about this feeling. He had followed Moses his entire adult life; learned under him, served him, and watched how he led. Then Moses was gone, the Jordan River was in front of him, and God handed him a territory with no map and no predecessor to ask. The mission was clear. The path was not.

The word God gave Joshua wasn't a bulletproof strategy. It was a way of being:

"Be strong and courageous. Do not be afraid; do not be discouraged, for the LORD your God is with you wherever you go." Joshua 1:9

Not once you have a plan. Not once you feel ready. Now.

You don't need a five-year plan to step forward. You just need to be strong and courageous. And what you have is the same thing Joshua had: the assurance that the One who does have a plan is already walking ahead of you into every single day of this.

The wide-open space is the doorway into a chapter of your life that has been waiting for you to have the time and the freedom to actually show up for it.

"What took me by surprise was the non-regimented life I was now facing. I'm the type of person who likes a schedule, so not following ANY schedule was scary! I found my footing because we lived on a ranch that required some daily activity. I quickly became so busy on the ranch; and I found a purpose!" — Pam S.

This Week's Activity

Read Joshua 1 as if the words were written for you. Through the eyes of this passage, think of something small you'd like to do that you have not had space for while you were working. Let that one thing be today's evidence that the wide-open calendar is a gift.

Optional Radiance Journal Prompts

- When in your life have you felt adrift before, and what did God do with that feeling? What did you learn from it?
- Joshua was told to be strong and courageous before he had crossed a single step of new territory. Are you following that instruction?
- What is one thing the wide-open calendar could give

you time for today that your working life never could?

Lord, the open calendar feels lonelier than I expected. I built my life around knowing what came next, and now I'm no longer sure about my future. Even though I have fewer responsibilities, some mornings I feel lost. So I'm taking You at Your word: be strong and courageous, because You are with me wherever I go. Help me trust that You've already been into this territory. Help me to feel Your presence with me. In Jesus' name, Amen.

If you love where this devotional is headed, would you consider leaving a short review? Your words are so important to helping the bookstore understand who else needs to see this book. Thank you~ Scan this QR code.

"Do not be conformed to this world, but be transformed by the renewing of your mind. Then you will be able to test and approve what is the good, pleasing, and perfect will of God." Romans 12:2

While a wide-open calendar feels free, it can feel intimidating. It's up to you to figure out how to spend your day. It can also feel lonely. Especially if no one has needed you for three days straight.

You may feel invisible even in a crowd — passed over in conversation, overlooked at a family gathering. And, you might start wondering, "Do I still matter?"

In her book *Get Out of Your Head*, Jennie Allen writes about the spiral: how a single anxious thought pulls you down into a pattern of believing things about yourself that are not true. She shows that the battle for your life is fought primarily in your mind. The lies we believe take root in our minds because they feel familiar; that lie feels true because it has so much evidence to support it. Allen's core argument, like Paul's in Romans 12, is that what is familiar is not the same as truth. Paul calls this the renewed mind of Romans 12:2 — a mind that recognizes the lie and replaces it with the truth of what God says about you.

Be transformed by the renewing of your mind. Paul isn't encouraging us to give platitudes about what's happening. He's talking about moving from the world's measuring

system to God's. And the world's measuring system, if you've spent any time in it, runs almost entirely on output. What did you produce? What did you contribute? What are you worth based on what you delivered?

God's measuring system has never once included a column for output.

This Week's Activity

Draw two columns on a blank page. Label the left column The World's Evidence and the right column God's Evidence.

In the left column, list every way you have been measuring your significance; things like your education, your job, the place you worked, your city, your family, and the house you live in.

In the right column, write the corresponding truth from Scripture that measures the same thing differently. Scripture defines your identity in Christ as a new creation. Here is a list to get you started:

I am a child of God. John 1:12
I am a new creation in Christ. 2 Corinthians 5:17
I am fully redeemed and forgiven. Ephesians 1:7
I am chosen to be holy and blameless before Him.
Ephesians 1:4
I am free from condemnation in Christ Jesus. Romans 8:1

I am complete in Him. Colossians 2:10
I am a member of Christ's body. 1 Corinthians 12:27
I am God's workmanship, created for good works.
Ephesians 2:10

Repeat these promises whenever you start spiraling; write it by hand so that your true identity becomes the familiar thought your mind reaches for.

Optional Radiance Journal Prompts

- Has the "Do I still matter?" question shown up for you?
- How did you know you mattered during your working years? What was the evidence you relied on?
- What steps can you take to replace untrue familiar thoughts with what God says is true about you?
- How would your days change if you fully believed what God says is the only thing that matters?

Prayer

Lord, I've been waiting to feel significant based on whether someone needed me today. Renew my mind. Help me see myself the way You see me. Help me to stop valuing my worth by what I do and how much money I have in the bank, but as someone You made and love and have never stopped calling by name. In Jesus' name, Amen.

Week 6: The Hidden Thread

When you look back over the years of your life, it can sometimes feel as though the story is a series of disconnected chapters: A job ends, we downsize, friendships fade, children grow up and begin their own lives. At the time, each event can feel abrupt or even disorienting. A door closes, and it's easy to view even these natural progressions as loss.

There are moments when you look back at times that felt like loss, and now, through the filter of time, you can see an unseen hand orchestrating it all for good. Through time, we can begin to see a hidden thread running through every chapter of the story. God is still weaving. Scripture gives us a glimpse of how He works in Isaiah 42:16.

What once looked like disconnected moments forms a pattern under God's hands. The experiences, lessons, relationships, and even the losses have all been part of something larger. Our lives have never been a series of accidents. They have been guided. They have been shaped. The quiet faithfulness of God has held them together. The Bible tells us that long before we ever held a job title, God already knew us and had a purpose for our lives. Retirement doesn't break that thread. In many ways, it allows us to see it more clearly.

"The hard things in life give the most valuable and important lessons." — Ruth A.

This Week's Activity

Look back over the milestones of your life, both painful and joyful. For each one, write what it gave you and what you learned. This might take some time; give yourself a few weeks if you need to.

Optional Radiance Journal Prompts

- What is one chapter of your life that felt like it was the worst possible outcome? Where can you see God's hand in it now?
- Where do you see God's leading most clearly when you look backward?
- What has the hard thing given you that the easy path never could have?

Prayer

Lord, I can barely see the beautiful tapestry You are creating, but I know enough about You to believe that You are creating something beautiful. There are so many chapters I wish I could have skipped if You had let me. But I'm trying to trust You; nothing was wasted. Thank You for leading me through the unfamiliar paths. Thank You for making darkness light, even when I couldn't see You doing it. Help me trust that what looks like a mess is in Your capable hands. In Jesus' name, Amen.

> *"I am the vine and you are the branches. The one who remains in Me, and I in him, will bear much fruit. For apart from Me you can do nothing." John 15:5*

All your life, you've worked for a title; your achievements in school and at work were organized around the goal of advancement. God sees it differently; He's invited you to an eternal harvest. The title kept you busy enough that the deeper question, "What am I actually here for?" got pushed to the side.

In John 15, Jesus is at the table with His closest friends, the night before He was crucified, and He chooses this image: the vine and the branches. Your professional title described what you did. The vine describes how you were always meant to live, as a branch drawing everything it needs from the source of all life.

You have never been the one who produced the fruit: the branch doesn't strain to grow grapes. It doesn't hold strategy sessions about the harvest. It doesn't hustle. It stays connected, and life flows through it. Fruit is the natural result of that connection.

That is a completely different relationship to productivity than the one we've lived by. Output was something you generated through effort, discipline, and long hours. John 15 describes fruit as the overflow of connection. You still have that one single job: to stay connected to the vine. Everything else follows.

The world's economy of production said your best years were those with the longest hours and the highest output.

God's economy says your best fruit grows when you are most connected and resting in Him.

"I kept thinking useful would feel like something official. Then I realized I'd been standing at my neighbor's fence chatting for over an hour and neither of us wanted to go inside. And being there for each other, listening, was the most important thing in the world." — Evelyn P.

This Week's Activity

What's the one area of your life where you feel most alive, most genuinely yourself? When an hour feels like ten minutes. Ask the Holy Spirit specifically: "Where do You want me to focus my time and energy, based on where my passions actually are?"

Optional Radiance Journal Prompts

- Where have you been trying to produce fruit through effort and willpower rather than connection?
- Jesus says, "Apart from Me, you can do nothing." Where has trying to make things happen produced nothing lasting?
- What would your days look like if staying connected to the vine was the primary thing?

Prayer

Lord, I've been acting like my worth is what I produce, and I'm tired of trying to prove myself. Teach me what it feels like to stop straining and start receiving. Show me how to rest in You, and to let Your Spirit work through me in how

to give to others. In Jesus' name, Amen.

Week 8: Hidden With Christ

David was a man who knew what it felt like to be overlooked, dismissed, and forgotten by the institutions that once celebrated him. When he wrote Psalm 17, he wasn't asking God to restore his visibility in the world. He was asking to be seen by God. Psalm 17:8 answers that feeling with these words: "the apple of Your eye" and "hidden in the shadow of Your wings."

David's prayer in Psalm 17 echoes what Paul later declares in Colossians 3:3. Being hidden with Christ means living from the security of being completely known and held by the One whose opinion of you has never depended on what you produced or the title you carried.

Retirement has a way of stripping the armor off, whether you planned for it or not. The world may see you differently now. God sees you the same way He always has. As the apple of His eye, held close, and known completely.

"I highly recommend planning a reset trip within the first year of your retirement. Nobody we met on our reset trip cared what jobs we used to have. You'll make new friends and start a fresh new life." —
Dawn M.

This Week's Activity

Write a letter this week to yourself, from God, based on

Psalm 17:8.

- How have you noticed that your friends and family have a new, revised view of you, and in what ways?
- What does it mean to be hidden with Christ?
- David wrote Psalm 17 amid real threats and real dismissal. Where do you need his prayer most?

Lord, I'll admit that being less visible than I used to be is harder than I expected. I didn't know how much of my sense of being seen was tied to the role. So I'm asking You, as David did, to keep me as the apple of Your eye. Hide me under the shadow of Your wings. Help me to trust that being known by You is the only thing that was ever real. In Jesus' name, Amen.

> *"But now, this is what the LORD says— He who created you, O Jacob, and He who formed you, O Israel: 'Do not fear, for I have redeemed you; I have called you by your name; you are Mine!'" Isaiah 43:1*

In Isaiah 43, there are three phrases and twelve words. Every single one of them is personal. God speaks of ownership in the warm, specific language of a relationship that predates every title you have ever held. I have called you by your name. You are Mine.

The God who flung the stars into place, who holds the oceans in His hands, who was and is and is to come, knows your name. The specific name that belongs only to you, not to your role, your reputation, or your LinkedIn profile.

Called by name. Redeemed. His. That is who you are when every title has been set down. That is who you have always been.

> *"Everyone told me to enjoy the freedom. And I did, for about six weeks. Then I needed to figure something out. Retirement from something is just an ending. You need to move yourself toward something." — Marge T.*

This Week's Activity

If you don't have a "life verse" yet, pray and ask the Holy Spirit to bring a verse to your heart. Let it reveal itself in God's time, let yourself be surprised at how He speaks to

you, and how it shows up.

Once you have it, write it on a card and put it somewhere you will see it every morning; the bathroom mirror, the kitchen window, or your phone's wallpaper. Better yet, commit to memorizing it. Whisper it to yourself as you fall asleep. Let it be the first true thing that comes to mind each day, before the world has a chance to offer you anything else.

- You are mine is present tense in Isaiah 43. Not *you were mine* when you were useful — but *You are Mine*, right now, exactly as you are. How does knowing that feel?
- Rewrite your life verse, or Isaiah 43:1, with your name, as if it's a personal letter to you.

Heavenly Father, You have been calling since before I was born. I want to live like that; it is the most important thing I know about myself. Help me hear You calling it this week. Bring this back to me: "I have called you by your name. You are Mine." That is enough. It has always been enough. In Jesus' name, Amen.

Week 10: Fearfully and Wonderfully Made

Psalm 139:14 is easy to believe at twenty-five. It asks considerably more of you after sixty-five, when your body is changing in ways you didn't choose. Fearfully and wonderfully made. Okay, but what about the knees? What about the way your mother's hands have appeared on the ends of your arms? What about the face in the morning that is beginning to look more like your history?

If only wrinkles and gray hair were the extent of it. Aging also brings harder realities: medical diagnoses that bring our mortality in full view; physical limitations that change how safe you feel moving through the day, and the appearance of pains in new places almost every day. "The length of our days is seventy years— or eighty if we are strong— yet their pride is but labor and sorrow" (Psalm 90:10). Yet even within that truth, the claim of Psalm 139 still stands: "I praise You, for I am fearfully and wonderfully made." (Psalm 139:14). The body that now carries signs of time is the same body God formed with care. And Scripture reminds us that our days have never been random: "Your eyes saw my unformed body; all my days were written in Your book and ordained for me before one of them came to be." (Psalm 139:16).

As the outer life changes, the inner life can deepen. Paul

writes, "Therefore we do not lose heart. Though our outer self is wasting away, yet our inner self is being renewed day by day." (2 Corinthians 4:16). The outer changes are real. The inner renewal is just as real. You don't have to pretend the changes aren't happening. You are invited to discover that the wonder God built into you isn't going to diminish with the years.

Psalm 139 is not a lament about accepting aging as inevitable; it is a celebration of astonishment and gratitude. My soul knows that very well, David writes, and he is not talking about reluctant acknowledgment. He is talking about wonder.

The most fully realized version of you is the one standing here now. Weathered and wise and completely, wholly His.

"At first, don't volunteer for every new thing that everyone invites you to do. Let your calendar evolve as you figure out how you want your life to feel day-to-day." — Chrissy T.

This Week's Activity

Go through your phone and delete junk photos, screenshots, duplicates, and especially the ones you just don't want to see anymore. Likely, there's a lot of junk, so don't expect to complete this in one sitting. Just make it a new practice in your monthly or weekly routine.

As you go, favorite/heart the ones that make you laugh, that show you fully alive, that remind you of a time when you were completely yourself. If someone else is in the photo with you, send it to them with a note about how grateful you are for their presence in your life.

- David says his soul knows he is wonderfully made. What would it mean for your soul to know that?
- Try writing a poem about yourself, praising every wrinkle, scar, and gray hair you've earned. What if you were grateful for your body that has taken you this far, for all the work it's done?
- What do you love being able to do in the body you have? Write a list that has nothing to do with appearance and everything to do with aliveness.

Prayer

Lord, help me see what You see when You look at me. Not the version I was twenty years ago, not the version I'll be someday, but this one, exactly as I am now. You called me fearfully and wonderfully made. I want my soul to know that very well. Teach me to agree with You. In Jesus' name, Amen.

Week 11: The Strength of Solitude

Regardless of your life situation, retirement will require you to spend some time alone. How you feel about your own company matters more than most people will tell you.

For women who have enjoyed the busy day surrounded by colleagues, clients, family demands, and the steady hum of other people's needs, the increase in solitude can bring loneliness. You might have imagined it as restful and peaceful. Sometimes it is. But sometimes the stillness brings things up that you've buried.

Work friendships and the camaraderie of daily conversations in hallways, the small companionship of shared routines, and the sweetness of teamwork and goal accomplishments are gone. The structure that held those friendships together is now gone. We are made for connection: "Two are better than one... for if one falls down, his companion can lift him up!" (Ecclesiastes 4:9–10). Recognizing the loss of those daily connections is part of the adjustment. But loneliness can also be a sign that you need to create new pathways to bring new people into your world.

Loneliness is an invitation to rebuild new friendships with intention — and friendships rooted in mutual faith and shared values are a good place to start.

Retirement can also change the rhythm of a marriage. When a spouse who once left each morning is suddenly home all

day, the quiet patterns you built over the years may need to be gently reworked. Shared space requires grace. Inner peace stays with you even when you are with someone; it is cultivated with intention and communicated with kindness. Scripture reminds us, "Each of you should look not only to your own interests, but also to the interests of others" (Philippians 2:4). In this season, learning to honor one another's need for both connection and quiet becomes part of loving well. Solitude strengthens you personally, and that strength makes renegotiation gentler rather than tense.

Solitude is not the same thing as loneliness. Loneliness is the ache of unwanted isolation. Solitude is the intentional practice of being present with yourself and with God, without the noise of the world filling in all the gaps. One is something that happens to you. The other is something you cultivate, and the cultivation takes time, patience, and a willingness to sit with the discomfort until it becomes something else entirely.

Zephaniah 3:17 is a remarkable verse for this particular week. God rejoices over you with singing. God is quieting you with His love. We do not have a distant God issuing directives from a safe remove. We have a God who draws close, who delights, who sings. When you learn to be still enough to receive that, solitude stops feeling like a void and starts feeling like a dwelling place.

This is true whether you live alone or have a house full of family members. The practice of solitude is not about the number of people in the room. It is about learning to find your own center when the noise clears, and discovering what the center holds. Your identity is secure regardless of who is in the room with you, because you are in God's good

company.

Yet, human connection is a great source of vitality. The strength you build in solitude is not meant to replace relationships; it is meant to make you more fully present for them. The woman who knows how to be alone and at peace with herself tends to show up differently in her relationships. She brings something whole rather than looking for someone else to fill in the missing pieces.

> *"I used to turn the TV on the second I walked in the door, just for noise. It took me a long time to stop doing that. Now I actually like my house quiet. I think God was in there the whole time, waiting for me to stop filling up all the space." — Jackie M.*

This Week's Activity

Go to a movie or out to dinner by yourself this week. Leave your phone in your bag. Practice being present with your own thoughts and with God in a public setting, without filling the space with scrolling or distraction.

At the end of the week, reach out to one person for a simple, real conversation. Let the solitude and the connection balance each other. Notice what each one gives you that the other can't.

Optional Radiance Journal Prompts

- Does being alone feel like rest, discomfort, or both?
- What is the difference, in your own experience, between loneliness and solitude? Have you felt both since retirement began? Describe what each one feels like from the inside.

- Zephaniah 3:17 describes God rejoicing over you and quieting you with His love. What would it take to receive that truth in the stillness, rather than rushing to fill the stillness with noise?

Prayer

Lord, teach me to love solitude because I know You are in it. Help me sit in the stillness without rushing to fill it. In those mornings when the quiet feels more like absence than presence, remind me of this: You are here. You are rejoicing over me. You are singing. Let me be still enough to hear it. In Jesus' name, Amen.

Week 12: Be Still and Know

The shortest verse in this entire devotional, and quite possibly the most countercultural version of life we know today. "Be still and know that I am God."

You've been trained to pack as much as possible into the day before noon; stillness may not come easily. But Scripture is giving us a command with a promise built right into it. The knowing is on the other side of the stillness. You don't get there by thinking harder or doing more. You get there by stopping.

That is genuinely countercultural. The world has never once told you that stillness is productive. Every device you own is engineered to prevent stillness. Most of us check our phones within minutes of waking — meaning the first voice we hear belongs to the news cycle, the inbox, or someone else's curated version of their life. God's voice tends to require more space than that.

> *"I like to give myself the first hour of the day without the news, or distractions. Just me, Jesus and my journal. The first morning I did this was not easy – I kept wanting to check the news. By the third morning, I stretched it into two hours – just didn't want the peacefulness to end. Now, I have to tell my kids not to worry about me for the first two hours of the day if I don't text them back!" — Melissa R.*

If you have not yet picked up the journaling habit from Week 1, this is a good time to re-evaluate it. If you are journaling,

here's some more evidence to help you keep the habit: Journaling is a powerful way to help you get a bird's-eye view of what God might be doing in your life. Adele Calhoun writes in Spiritual Disciplines Handbook that journaling is, at its root, an act of paying attention; noticing where God is moving. It can reveal ideas, spark your intuition, and show you how your life is turning out much better than you thought. You only need something to write with, paper, and the willingness to tell the truth on the page.

This Week's Activity

Do a real digital declutter this week. Turn off push notifications. Delete apps you haven't opened in three months. Unsubscribe from every email list that shows up in your inbox and doesn't feed your soul.

This is not a one-time event. Return to the declutter regularly. Clearing the digital noise is part of clearing space for the life you actually want to be living.

Optional Radiance Journal Prompts

- What is the first thing you reach for in the morning, and what does that tell you about what you believe you need before the day begins?
- Psalm 46:10 says the knowing comes through the stillness. What is something you have been trying to figure out through thinking that you might need to receive through being still?

Prayer

Lord, I want to be someone who starts the day with You rather than with the noise. Help me build this practice. Help me protect the first minutes of my morning the way I would protect anything else that matters to me. On the mornings when I reach for the phone before I reach for You, have mercy on me, and call me back to Yourself. Meet me in the stillness. In Jesus' name, Amen.

> *"'Why were you looking for Me?' He asked. 'Did you not know that I had to be in My Father's house?'" Luke 2:49*

Luke 2:49 holds the first recorded words of Jesus in Scripture—spoken after His parents had been frantically searching for Him for three days, convinced something had gone terribly wrong. They found Him exactly where He was supposed to be, doing exactly what He was meant to do, completely at home in His Father's house.

Jesus wasn't just talking about a location—He was revealing identity. He knew who His Father was, and because of that, He knew where He belonged. In other words, His identity determined His placement. And that's where this meets you.

When you don't know who you are, your time gets filled by whatever feels urgent. But when you begin to understand who you are—who you belong to—your life starts to align differently. You don't just drift into your days. You begin to choose them.

So the question isn't just, "What will I do today?" It's deeper than that: Do you know who you are well enough to choose where you belong?

What will you do with the time you've been given? Not just practically—but intentionally. Not just reactively—but from identity.

Over the first thirteen weeks of this journey, you've begun to uncover who you are without your title. And what you've been discovering, week by week, is this: you are far more

interesting, more deeply loved, and more purposeful than any job description could ever capture:

- You are God's handiwork.
- You were known before you were hired.
- You are called by name.
- You are the apple of His eye.
- You are fearfully and wonderfully made.
- You are a branch connected to the vine.
- You are learning to be still and receive what has been waiting for you in the stillness all along.

None of this is new information about you. It has always been true. You just finally have the time and the space to believe it.

"My life today feels so rewarding and full that I wonder how I ever found time to work." — Faye W.

Write your Awaken Declaration; two or three sentences. Start with: "I used to believe," and end with: "Now I know." When you read it again at the end of Week 52, you will barely recognize the woman who wrote it.

- Looking back over the last thirteen weeks, what is the biggest shift in how you see yourself?
- Jesus, at twelve years old, was completely certain of His belonging, even when everyone around Him thought something had gone wrong. What are you certain about yourself?

Lord, thirteen weeks ago, I wasn't sure who I was going to be on this side of the title. I'm starting to find out, and what I'm finding is better than I expected. Thank You for every hard week. Thank You for every morning I showed up to the stillness and found You already there. I don't want to lose what You've been building in me. In Jesus' name, Amen.

Phase Two: Flourish – Weeks 14–26

Lamentations 3:22–23 · Hosea 14:5 · Psalm 92:14

Phase Two is called Flourish because flourishing is what happens when a plant stops being transplanted and starts being watered. God's faithfulness arrives every single morning like dew, whether you notice it or not. Over the next thirteen weeks, you will learn to receive what God has already placed at your feet before the day begins. You will practice the morning stillness, build the discipline of joy, and discover that the renewal He promises is not dramatic or sudden. It is gentle, daily, and completely sufficient. The lily does not force its own opening. It receives the dew, and in time, it blooms.

Refer to your Free Gift Map through the QR code.

"Because of the loving devotion of the LORD we are not consumed, for His mercies never fail. They are new every morning; great is Your faithfulness!" Lamentations 3:22–23

This week's verse was written in the midst of rubble, in the wreckage of Jerusalem after everything had fallen apart. The city was destroyed, the temple gone, the people scattered. It is spoken while everything appears to be falling apart.

If you read the entire chapter, you'll find a long lament, just as the title says, about the devastation of Jerusalem. Amid the pain, the writer pauses to say: His mercies never fail. They are new every morning. Great is His faithfulness.

Even when your world falls apart, or life as you know it ends, God's faithfulness doesn't.

Phase Two is called Flourish because flourishing is a sign of growth; when a plant stops being transplanted and starts being watered. You have been transplanted. Thirteen weeks of new soil, new rhythms, new questions about who you are. Now the water comes. Every morning. Fresh. Already there.

The beautiful part of this verse is that it doesn't ask you to pretend that everything is fine when it isn't. There will be days when your morning feels like rubble; nights when you wrestle with worry. This verse is not asking you to pretend otherwise; instead, it asks you to look for what is new. The mercy is there whether you feel it or not. The practice is the stillness; God does the revealing.

"I spent the first two weeks sleeping in and calling it rest. I'm sure I needed it. Now, I still don't set an alarm, but I wake up early on my own just because I like the quiet time with my Bible." — Bette H.

This Week's Activity

Leonardo da Vinci once wrote that when a tree trunk splits into branches, the combined strength of those branches equals the strength of the trunk beneath them. The life flowing through the tree is not lost when it spreads out—it flows through all of it.

Follow a branch with your eyes from where it meets the trunk all the way out to the smallest twig. That same life is flowing through every part of it. The branch doesn't generate that life. It doesn't try harder to grow leaves or bear weight. It simply stays connected—and because it is connected, it is strong.

Now consider your own life. Where have you been trying to carry strength on your own, as if it depends on you? Where have you been acting like a branch disconnected from the source? You are not the source of your strength. You are connected to it.

Optional Radiance Journal Prompts

- Where do you still catch yourself trying to earn the morning, performing rather than receiving? What does that habit feel like in your body?
- Lamentations was written from rubble. When has His mercy shown up for you in a time that felt like wreckage?
- Phase Two is called Flourish. What does flourishing

look like for you specifically?

Lord, thank You that I don't need everything in my life to be perfect to receive Your mercies. Thank You that Your faithfulness was already here before I opened my eyes. Help me build a practice that honors that. Help me guard the first part of my day for You, because I have found out what's on the other side of the stillness, and I don't want to miss it. Great is Your faithfulness. I am learning to live in that truth. In Jesus' name, Amen.

Week 15: Fresh and Renewed

"I will be like the dew to Israel; he will blossom like the lily and take root like the cedars of Lebanon." Hosea 14:5

Hosea 14:5 gives us an image of God that is unlike almost any other in Scripture.

Not a consuming fire. Not a mighty fortress. Not a refining flame. Not a rushing wind. Dew. The lily in this verse does not force its own flowering. It does not strategize about how to bloom or create a timeline for its own growth. It receives what falls on it each morning, and it opens its petals.

The dew metaphor is exactly how God's daily renewal operates. His mercies from Week 14, His faithfulness, this gentle and persistent making-new won't be instantaneous. It won't feel like anything is happening. But the lily is growing. The roots are going deeper. The blooming is coming.

There are times when you look at yourself and compare yourself to other people, and think, "I should have all of this figured out by now." Or maybe you feel like the time you've spent in this book should be more obviously transformative by now. You showed up for Week 1 expecting a dramatic reinvention and found something slower and quieter instead. That's how our powerful God works.

Your effort is not needed for God to work; accepting that truth requires you to go against what our culture has taught us most of our lives. You do not have to manufacture your gifts; you simply have to receive what God is already building in you every single morning, just for you.

"Keep a running list of everything you've always said you'd do someday and get them scheduled." — Joyce A.

This Week's Activity

When Jesus said, I am the vine, you are the branches, He was showing that the branches don't produce life on their own. Life comes from the trunk or vine. The branches extend and distribute what is already flowing through the main source.

This week, instead of trying to do more, practice noticing your connection. At three points during your day—morning, afternoon, and evening—pause for one minute and ask: "Am I connected right now, or am I striving?"

Optional Radiance Journal Prompts

- What is one thing that is blooming in your life that had no room to grow during your working years? Describe it specifically.
- Where have you been trying to force your own growth or manufacture your own transformation rather than receiving what God is already bringing? What would it feel like to stop?

Prayer

Lord, thank You for being the kind of God who shows up as dew. I don't always know what to do with that; the world has trained me in the dramatic, obvious transformation I could measure. Help me trust Your slow, quiet work. Help me receive the daily, faithful, unhurried renewal You are

already bringing and to stop trying to hurry what You have designed to take the time it takes. I trust the blooming to You. In Jesus' name, Amen.

> *"Rejoice in the Lord always. I will say it again: Rejoice!"*
> *Philippians 4:4*

Paul says it twice because he knows you missed it the first time. He knows exactly how fast that instruction starts to feel impossible under the strain of everyday life, and how much we are going to need the reminder.

When I think of joy in the darkness, I think of Corrie ten Boom. She was a Dutch watchmaker's daughter who was arrested by the Nazis in 1944 for hiding Jewish families in her home. She survived the Ravensbrück concentration camp—smuggling pages from the Gospel of John inside her dress—watched her sister Betsie die there. She later wrote in her book *The Hiding Place*, "There is no pit so deep that God's love is not deeper still."

The words on those pages of the Gospel of John gave her strength and comfort. She was able to choose joy not because her circumstances were bearable, but because she had decided that joy was not something circumstances could give or take away.

Both Paul and Corrie understood that joy is not a feeling you wait for—it is something you cultivate.

Yes, we do have to train our eyes to see the joy that is already around us. Just as negativity rubs off when you spend time with negative people, so does joy. And joy is a choice. The more you choose joy, the more that "joy" becomes your default reaction, regardless of what is happening around

you. You are a person who can practice joy, who can get better at it, and who can train herself to see God's goodness in the details of an ordinary day.

"I made a playlist of every song that reminds me of good times from my life. When I hear them, they take me back to some of the happiest moments of my life, and that happiness takes over my day." — Dottie K.

Pay attention to the gifts God has given you; they're there on purpose, and so is your ability to enjoy them. The Bible tells us, "Every good and perfect gift is from above, coming down from the Father of the heavenly lights," (James 1:17).

In The Weight of Glory, C.S. Lewis argued that our longing for beauty and pleasure is never really about the thing itself. The pleasure is more like a scent — evidence of a flower we haven't yet found. What we are chasing, even when we don't know it, is the source of all beauty, and that source is God.

Paul's instruction to rejoice always is not to paint every discomfort with a pink paintbrush. It's a call to take control of your mind. The God-centered desires that fill you up are God speaking to you in a very personal way. Pay attention to them.

The God who purposely hung the stars also thought to make the coffee delightful, the music beautiful, and a good laugh with a friend feel like medicine.

"Everyone at your job will manage just fine without you; now you must learn to be 'just fine' without the job."— Carol Anne W.

This Week's Activity

Make a playlist this week of music that genuinely sparks joy. Sing along, and even dance to it. Make this a daily habit.

Start a gratitude journal or a joy log, and make lists. Train your mind and your eye to see the good in ordinary moments.

Optional Radiance Journal Prompts

- Do you think your friends consider you a joyful person?
- Paul wrote, "Rejoice always" from prison. What is the hardest circumstance in which you have managed to find genuine joy? What made it possible?
- Have you been treating delight as a reward you haven't earned yet, or a distraction from more serious things? What would change if you treated it as a discipline instead?

Prayer

Lord, I want to be a joyful woman, rather than someone who needs everything to be perfect first. The kind of woman who can feel and see your goodness even when the circumstances look bleak. Train my eyes. Help me find You in the details of the ordinary day, in the music and the morning, and the things that make me feel alive. Thank You for putting delight inside me. I don't want to leave that gift unopened. In Jesus' name, Amen.

Week 17: Inwardly Renewed

Yes, our bodies are giving us new messages about our mortality. Paul knew that nothing could fix what was inevitably happening to our bodies. Not even the right eye cream can fix it!

But, still, even with the biological changes, we are being *renewed day by day*. It's always happening, each day, in the same way the dew arrives every morning without asking permission. You don't manufacture it. You receive it.

2 Corinthians 4:16 is a promise for the woman who keeps showing up. The outward is changing, yes. The inward woman is being renewed every single day. The journal is just where you get to watch it happen.

"Try writing your prayers instead of just thinking about them. It's amazing how organized and less stressed you will feel. Since I started doing it, I can see how God is actually moving in my life, and it builds my faith." — Miriam O.

This week, make a conscious effort to write your prayers, as a letter:

> *Dear Father, here is what is on my mind this morning. Here is what I am grateful for, and here is what I am still afraid of. Here is what I read in Your Word this week, and here is the question it left me with.*

Begin each entry with a Scripture, and then tie your requests to one of His promises.

- What is one thing you have been wanting to have a conversation with God about? Write it down, and wait for the Holy Spirit to answer you. Some people use their non-dominant hand to write the answer.
- Paul says the inward person is being renewed day by day. Where do you see evidence of that renewal in yourself, even if it's small?
- What is one request you have been carrying, and what is the specific promise from Scripture you are going to tie it to this week?

Lord, I want to bring You the real version of what's inside me, not the edited one. Help me write my way to You this week with nothing held back. You already know what's there. I just want to stop pretending I can manage it without saying it. Renew what is inside me, day by day, the way only You can. I'm showing up on the page. Meet me there. In Jesus' name, Amen.

"Who satisfies you with good things, so that your youth is renewed like the eagle's." Psalm 103:5

Eagles go through a fascinating process called molting. They shed outer layers that are heavy, worn out, and broken to make room for the new. When they emerge, they aren't just survivors; they are actually stronger and more capable than they were before. Psalm 103:5 tells us that God is doing that exact work in us. He satisfies our souls with good things so that our vitality is renewed.

In her book, *The Faith to Flourish*, Christine Caine writes about how we often want to skip the middle of the race and get straight to the trophy. But she reminds us that the middle is where our muscles are built. It is where we learn that we can do hard things through Christ. Even now, in this new chapter, you are still building spiritual muscle. You are running a race that is less about speed and more about steady, joyful faithfulness.

This isn't a promise about finding a fountain of youth or pretending your knees don't click when you stand up. Renewal doesn't mean God is restoring you to who you were at twenty-five. Why would we want to go back there anyway? We've worked too hard for this wisdom! Instead, He is making you genuinely new, carrying forward the best of your history while releasing the weights that no longer serve you.

For too long, we've been running on the adrenaline of deadlines and the demands of others. That kind of energy is brittle. The vitality God offers you today is radiant and

rooted. It is the strength to say yes to what matters and the peace to enjoy the life He has carefully planned for you. You are shedding the forced effort to become the woman who can truly soar.

"I stopped fighting the mirror somewhere around sixty-eight. Not because I gave up, but because I finally got tired of being at war with someone God made. That felt like the more faithful thing." —
Harriet B.

This Week's Activity

Research shows that strength training for women our age helps protect bone density, keeps us strong, and even helps keep our brains sharp. If you aren't in a strength training program, pick one way to challenge your muscles. It doesn't have to be a gym membership. It could be ten minutes of hand weights while you watch the news, a beginner exercise video, or even some intentional gardening. Start small, but start. Ask your doctor what's right for you, find a class you enjoy, or pull up a beginner workout on YouTube. Your body is God's temple, and keeping it strong is an act of worship, not of vanity.

Optional Radiance Journal Prompts

- What's the first image that comes to mind when you hear the word vitality? How do you think that definition has changed from what you thought in your twenties?
- What are the worn-out "feathers" you need to shed this week? These could be old habits of worry, a need to prove your worth, or physical clutter that weighs

you down.

- Psalm 103:5 says God satisfies our desires with good things. What is one good thing you have discovered recently that makes you feel energized?
- How does the image of an eagle soaring change the way you view your physical aging?

Lord, I've spent a lot of years feeling like my energy was a finite resource I had to manage and ration. Thank You for the promise that You are the one who renews me. Help me to shed what is heavy and old so I can receive the fresh strength You have for me today. Teach me to soar rather than just shuffle through my day. I want to be more fully alive than I have ever been. Renew my heart and my body for Your glory. In Jesus' name, Amen.

"This is the day that the LORD has made; we will rejoice and be glad in it." Psalm 118:24

When Psalm 118 declares, "This is the day that the LORD has made," it celebrates the moment after God's rescue, when a season of danger is finally replaced with the joy of deliverance. Trouble came, yes. But now, the trouble has already passed, and the psalmist was celebrating the day God finally brought him through it.

God does intervene and change the outcome, but do you stop to recognize God's hand after the storm has cleared? When the disease is managed, when the money comes, or when opportunity opens up after a drought, those moments are not accidents. Scripture presents them as days God has shaped and brought about.

Week 16 invited us to cultivate a posture of gratitude; this verse goes one step further — it's an invitation to notice *when* God has stepped in and to respond with joy.

God made your heart and mind to work better when you are thankful. Two experts, Robert Emmons and Michael McCullough, conducted research to see what happens when people focus on their blessings. Their findings were compiled into a report titled *Counting Blessings Versus Burdens.* The results are not a surprise. The people who counted blessings had more energy and felt much better than those who only thought about their problems. They even slept better. The psalmist didn't just count blessings, he named the One who made the day that held them.

This Week's Activity

Pull out the joy log or gratitude journal you started back in Week 16, and add to it in a new way. Instead of only looking for big, exciting moments, deliberately start looking for the small hidden mercies in the trials.

Optional Radiance Journal Prompts

- How has your idea of a good day changed since you stopped working?
- When you look back on a difficult time from your past, do you see now how God was carrying you through it?
- If you really believed that today was a special gift made just for you, how would that change the way you spend your afternoon?

Prayer

Lord, I want to see my life the way You see it. Help me to stop looking for what is missing and start noticing all the ways You are taking care of me. Thank You for this day, not because it's perfect, but because You are the one who made it. Help my eyes to see the small, hidden gifts You put in my path today. I want to be a woman who is known for her thankful heart. In Jesus' name, Amen.

Week 20: Still Bearing Fruit

"In old age they will still bear fruit; healthy and green they will remain." Psalm 92:14

That word "still" is doing a lot of heavy lifting in this verse. It doesn't say you used to bear fruit back when you had a desk and a title. It says you are doing it, in the present tense, while your calendar is wide open and your leadership roles have vanished. The Bible describes you, as you age, as vibrant, full of life, and still producing.

In nature, a tree that is full of sap is alive and flexible. It's the opposite of a brittle, dead stick that snaps in the wind. Being green means you are still growing and producing something of value. Even as you age, you are a living, breathing part of God's garden.

God does not move us into a new chapter to let us wither; He moves us so we can cast a different kind of shade and feed a different generation.

When you share what you've learned, you are planting seeds that will grow long after you're gone. It's a way of making sure your life remains full of sap because you are pouring that life into someone else.

"Your best years for helping others aren't behind you; they are happening because you finally have the time to sit down and really listen." — Michelle W.

One of the most beautiful ways to bear fruit is through mentoring. You have wisdom that a younger woman is currently praying for. Maybe it's a neighbor overwhelmed with toddlers, a granddaughter trying to figure out her faith, or a younger woman just starting her career. You don't need a fancy certificate to help them; you just need your God-given testimony and a willing heart.

Optional Radiance Journal Prompts

- What does it feel like to know God describes you as green and full of sap?
- How do you think the Holy Spirit is giving you new life?
- What is one thing you know now that you wish you had known thirty years ago?

Prayer

Lord, thank You that I am still bearing fruit. Thank You that You don't see me as someone who is winding down, but as someone who is still growing. Help me to stay flexible and full of life. Show me who needs the wisdom You've given me. Help me to be a good listener and a faithful friend to the women coming up behind me. I want my life to bring You glory by showing others how good You are. In Jesus' name, Amen.

"The righteous will flourish like a palm tree, and grow like a cedar in Lebanon." Psalm 92:12

The psalmist chose these two trees for a very good reason: Palm trees and the cedars of Lebanon are both known for their endurance. A palm tree continues to produce fruit year after year, even in harsh conditions. The cedar of Lebanon, on the other hand, was famous for its height, strength, and longevity. Its wood was used in temples and palaces because it could last for generations.

Together, the two trees form a picture of a life that is both fruitful and steady. The palm tree suggests vitality and ongoing usefulness. The cedar suggests deep roots and strength that endures over time. Psalm 92 describes a life that continues to mature and remain productive long after the early seasons have passed.

That is why the psalm goes on to say that the righteous will still bear fruit in old age and remain "healthy and green." When someone is planted in God's presence, their usefulness does not expire with the passing of years. Their wisdom deepens, their perspective widens, and their influence often becomes quieter but stronger.

Your years of meaningful growth are not behind you; a life rooted in God does not slowly dry out. It continues to bear fruit, often in ways that were not possible in earlier, busier years.

Strength becomes steadiness. Activity becomes insight.

Experience becomes guidance for others. The psalmist teaches us that a life planted in the Lord continues to flourish.

"A career is only one tiny part of your identity. Your employer will move on without you; it's up to you to figure out how to move on without them." — Anne W.

This Week's Activity

Staying green is a choice that keeps us curious. Decide that there is still so much to see and understand about God's world. Learn something new this week that genuinely stretches you intellectually. Pick a topic that gives you a sense of wonder. Check out a book at the library to discover how a particular animal or ecosystem works, or look into the history of a civilization you know almost nothing about. If you want a scriptural deep dive, read Job 38-41. It contains some of the most vivid, astonishing descriptions of the natural world in all of ancient literature. It's God Himself describing the design of creation with an almost playful delight. Read those chapters and let yourself be genuinely surprised.

Optional Radiance Journal Prompts

- In what area of your life do you feel like you are growing the most?
- When was the last time you felt a true sense of wonder about the world God made?
- How does the image of a palm tree bending but not breaking change how you see your own struggles?
- What is one new ring of wisdom you have added to your life in this most recent year?

Lord, thank You for planting me in Your house. Thank You for continuing to grow me. Help me to stay curious and full of wonder at the world You have made. When the winds of life blow hard, help me to be like the palm tree, flexible and strong because I am rooted in Your love. Keep me green and vital so that I can show everyone around me how beautiful it is to grow old with You. In Jesus' name, Amen.

Week 22: The Path Shines Brighter

The world likes to call retirement the twilight years, which makes it sound like we are just waiting for the sun to go down for good. But God paints a very different picture. He says your path is like a sunrise that never stops rising. It doesn't dim; it actually gets stronger and clearer until it reaches the full light of noon.

If you are following Jesus, you aren't heading toward the shadows. You are heading toward the brightest light that exists. Every year you have lived has added another layer of light to your life. The wisdom you have gained, the kindness you have shown, and the way you have learned to trust God through the hard parts—all of that makes you more radiant now than you were at twenty. You are moving toward the best version of yourself.

In this part of your journey, you have a beautiful opportunity to change the way you talk about your life. We are tempted to spend so much time thinking about what we've lost – including our energy levels. But God invites us to look at the noon-day sun He is bringing us into. You are not fading. You are being revealed. The light is finally bright enough to see the real you, the one God planned for long before you ever had a resume.

"You have to make a conscious choice to be happy.
It's not something you wait to drop in your lap." —
Rose T.

Plant a small garden, or start a simple indoor herb garden on your windowsill. To germinate, seeds need the darkness beneath the soil. Only after that foundation is established does the small shoot begin to push upward through the soil.

Once the shoot is strong enough to break through the earth, almost imperceptibly, the light transforms the shoot into a plant. As in life, there are seasons when growth is happening beneath the surface; times when it looks as if God is silent, but He's forming roots of faith, patience, and wisdom. And just as a plant steadily moves toward the light, a life rooted in God continues moving toward the light. The path described in Proverbs 4:18 grows gradually until it finally breaks through the surface and reaches the sunlight.

- What is one thing you used to worry about in your career that the full light of retirement has shown wasn't that important after all?
- Who needs to hear a specific way you see God's light shining through them?

Lord, thank You for being the light on my path. I am so grateful that You don't see me as someone who is winding down, but as someone who is just reaching her full radiance. I want to be specific in my thanks and loud in my praise. Thank You for the abundance You have put right in front of me today. In Jesus' name, Amen.

Week 23: The Paycheck Was Never the Provider

"You may say in your heart, 'The power and strength of my hands have made this wealth for me.' But remember that it is the LORD your God who gives you the power to gain wealth," Deuteronomy 8:17–18

This is the first time in your adult life that the connection between your effort and your provision has stopped. For most of your adult life, financial security has been directly tied to effort. You worked, and the paycheck followed. You planned, and the bills were covered. Your labor produced the income that sustained your household.

And now that you've stopped working, where is your security? God knew you would have this fear, and He clearly addresses it back in Deuteronomy. There, God gives a clear warning against assuming that it has been your effort, not His, that allowed you to build wealth.

Even during the most productive years of your life, the real source of provision was never your job, your salary, or even your abilities. Those were the instruments. The power behind them came from God.

Then, look at how the Father and Jesus address this fear throughout Scripture:

- Jesus invites us to look at the natural world in Matthew 6:26: "Look at the birds of the air: They do not sow or reap or gather into barns, and yet your heavenly Father feeds them."

- David expresses the same confidence in Psalm 23:1: "The LORD is my shepherd; I shall not want." A shepherd is responsible for providing shelter, food, and safety for the sheep.
- Later in life, David reflects on his lifetime of experience and writes in Psalm 37:25: "I once was young and now am old, yet never have I seen the righteous abandoned or their children begging for bread."

These verses clearly establish God as your provider. But how are we to respond to Him? Here are two more verses that establish a clear foundation for us.

- Proverbs 3:9–10 says: "Honor the LORD with your wealth and with the firstfruits of all your crops; then your barns will be filled with plenty."
- In Malachi 3:10, God goes even further, saying: "Test Me in this" and "See if I will not open the windows of heaven and pour out for you blessing without measure."

These passages are often assumed to be about giving money, but the principle behind them goes much deeper than that. We honor God by bringing our whole selves to Him: He wants our hearts, our attention, and our time. Our honor shows up in the way we use our time, the attention we give Him in prayer, the love we extend to others, and the hospitality we offer through our homes. When our lives are oriented toward honoring Him first, generosity becomes a natural expression of trust. It is a way of acknowledging that everything we have—our resources, our abilities, and even our time—ultimately comes from Him.

When we live with open hands rather than clenched ones, we are acknowledging what Scripture teaches:

God has always been the provider. Work, opportunity, and income have been the tools He used in certain seasons. The source behind them has never changed.

When Paul wrote in Philippians 4:19, "And my God will supply all your needs according to His glorious riches in Christ Jesus," he was under house arrest in Rome, dependent on the generosity of other believers for support. The church in Philippi had just sent him a gift to help meet his needs, and Paul was writing to thank them. Right after acknowledging their generosity, he tells them that God will supply their needs as well.

"I spent years worrying about having enough to leave my kids in my will, but as I sat down to write this letter, I realized the 'gold' was the prayers I've prayed for them." —Bebe L.

Paul had learned something through experience: provision does not come from a job, a salary, or even careful planning. Those things may be the channels God uses in certain seasons, but they are not the source.

What is your first instinct when the number in your bank account stops going up and starts going down? Will you panic and give anxiety the wheel? The scripture in Deuteronomy reminds us of the source. Retirement strips away the delivery mechanism and asks you to trust the source directly.

This is not a book about budgeting, and this is not a week about financial planning. There are good advisors for that, and if you don't have one, finding one is wise stewardship.

This Week's Activity

Decide to collect something small and trivial. It could be a button, a paperclip, or a particular color of stone. It doesn't matter what it is. Every time you see the item you've chosen, pick it up and add it to a jar or bowl. Every time you add one, try to remember something that God has provided for you in valuable ways, but that wasn't tied to money; the neighbor who shoveled your driveway, the repairman who discovered a bigger problem and fixed it before it needed to be replaced, or the doctor who caught the disease in its early stages.

As your jar fills, you have a visible, tangible way to make Deuteronomy 8:18 a living testimony to God's faithfulness in providing for your every need.

Optional Radiance Journal Prompts

- How did you feel when the paycheck stopped?
- Looking at your provision list, what is the most unlikely way God has ever come through for you?
- Is there a difference between trusting God with your soul and trusting Him with your bank account? Where does that gap come from?
- What would change about your average week if you accepted that the source of your provision had not changed?

Lord, I'll be honest; the money fear is real, and some days it is loud. I did the responsible things, and I am grateful for that. But I can feel the difference now between trusting a paycheck and trusting You. I realize I may have confused the two for longer than I knew. So I'm bringing You the spreadsheet and the fear behind it. You have never once failed to provide what I actually needed. Help me build my confidence in that record rather than in the balance, which changes every month. You are the warehouse. Help me stop worrying about the truck. In Jesus' name, Amen.

Week 24: Those Who Look to Him Are Radiant

I'm sure you've seen those women; the ones who seem to glow from the inside out, the older they get. The glow they have doesn't come from a medi-spa; it's a deep, steady glow. The kind of radiance that can only come from looking at Him.

Interestingly, modern science has discovered something about the human face that makes this biblical image even more fascinating. Our faces are constantly revealing what we focus on and what we love. Over time, the muscles we use most often become the ones that shape our natural expression. A lifetime of worry tends to carve lines of tension into the skin. A lifetime of joy, gratitude, and peace creates a very different pattern. The face gradually reflects the heart's direction.

In other words, what we consistently look toward eventually shows up in how we look.

That is why the psalmist connects radiance with looking to God. A life spent turning toward Him, seeking His wisdom, remembering His faithfulness, and trusting Him through difficult seasons begins to change a person.

You may have thought your brightest years were behind you. Scripture promises the opposite. The more years a person

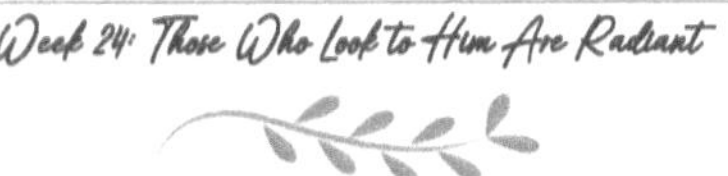

spends looking toward the Lord, the more opportunity there is for that steady radiance to grow.

"I assumed my mission was tied to my job. But it isn't about that. Life is more about how I love people and show up for them." — Carole A.

This Week's Activity

Before you do anything else, find a mirror. Look at your reflection and smile. Remind yourself that the woman looking back at you is fearfully and wonderfully made (Psalm 139:14).

Optional Radiance Journal Prompts

- Think of a woman you know — or once knew — who seems to glow with peace. What is it about the way she looks and carries herself?
- How does your posture change when you remember that you are God's workmanship, created for good works?

Prayer

Lord, I turn my face toward You today. I want my life to be a mirror that reflects Your goodness to everyone I meet. Thank You that I don't have to be young or successful in the world's eyes to be radiant. Wash away any old shame that makes me want to hide, and help me to stand tall as Your daughter. Teach me to recognize the moments when Your light is shining through me, and give me the words to speak life to those around me. In Jesus' name, Amen.

> *"Even to your old age, I will be the same, and I will bear you up when you turn gray. I have made you, and I will carry you; I will sustain you and deliver you." Isaiah 46:4*

There's a story told about a man who visited an elderly shepherd in the mountains of eastern Europe. The visitor noticed something curious about the shepherd's routine. Each evening, just before sunset, the man would gather his sheep and slowly lead them down a steep path toward a stone enclosure. One by one, the sheep grew tired from the climb and the long day of grazing. Eventually, the shepherd would bend down, lift the weakest ones onto his shoulders, and carry them the rest of the way home.

When the visitor asked why he did this every night, the shepherd smiled and said, "They follow all day while they are strong. But when they are tired, it is my turn to carry them."

Isaiah 46:4 captures that same picture of God's care. The verse uses four verbs to describe His relationship with us: made, bear, carry, and deliver. These are not past-tense promises that evaporate as we age.

Yet society would have us believe that heading into our later years will mean our support will diminish as well. This verse in Isaiah says the opposite. When your strength begins to fade, God steps forward. In fact, this verse emphasizes that His carrying becomes even more evident "even to your old age" and "when you turn gray."

One of the best ways to gauge whether you truly trust that promise is by observing your sleep. When you go to sleep, especially when your world might be falling apart, you are trusting God. He doesn't need you to keep the world spinning while you sleep. God is the one who sustains the universe while you rest. The psalmist puts it this way: "In vain you rise early and stay up late, toiling for bread to eat—for He gives sleep to His beloved" (Psalm 127:2).

> *"Since I can't do anything about the lines on my face, I might as well just think of them as maps of all the places God has walked with me. They are memories." — Martha J.*

This Week's Activity

Have you ever considered that sleep is an act of faith? Yet a good night's sleep is the first thing we lose when we are facing a crisis. "How can we possibly step away and sleep at a time like this?" It's as if we believe the resolution is in our hands, not God's. This week, start treating rest as a spiritual priority; a duty. Set a consistent bedtime, keep your room dark and cool, and put away all screens at least an hour before you plan to sleep. If you do find yourself awake at 3:00 a.m. with your mind spinning, start praying. Or get up and read your Bible, if you have to. Say, "Lord, You said You would carry this, so I'm handing it over now."

Optional Radiance Journal Prompts

- Which of those four verbs in Isaiah 46:4 — made, bear, carry, deliver — is the most welcoming reminder today, and why?
- How does the idea of sleep as an act of trust change the way you feel about your bedtime routine? About

your sleepless nights?

Lord, thank You for the promise that You will carry me even to my old age. I am so grateful that I don't have to be strong enough to hold everything together on my own. Help me to wear my years with honor, seeing them as the crown of glory You say they are. Teach me to rest deeply, trusting that the world stays in Your hands while I sleep. Show me the heavy things I've been lugging around that I no longer need to bear. I choose to let You carry me today. In Jesus' name, Amen.

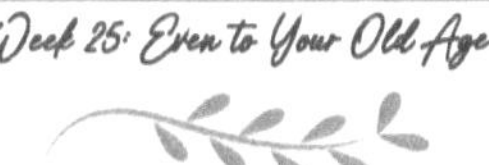

> *"But I am like an olive tree flourishing in the house of God;*
> *I trust in the loving devotion of God forever and ever."*
> *Psalm 52:8*

We have reached the end of Phase Two. For the last thirteen weeks, we have walked through the morning dew of God's mercy, learned to speak life over ourselves by uttering His promises, and practiced the holy discipline of rest. Today, we pause to mark what God has been doing in your heart.

Olive trees aren't known for being fast growers or having flashy, temporary flowers. They are famous for staying alive and strong for a very long time. Some of the most famous olive trees in the world have been standing for over a thousand years. They grow slowly, their trunks become silver with age, and—here is the best part—the fruit from the oldest trees is often the most prized. The richest, most flavorful oil comes from olives that have had the benefit of time.

You are that kind of tree. You have had time. You have deep roots that have held firm through many different kinds of weather. The world might prize things that are new or fast, but God prizes things that are evergreen and faithful.

David wrote this while his enemies were threatening everything he loved. He wasn't writing from peace; he was writing from trust. That's exactly what an olive tree in winter looks like; still green while everything around it has gone bare. The best fruit of your life is being pressed right now, and the oil it produces is more precious than anything you could have offered in your youth. You aren't just an

ornament in God's house; you are a living, breathing testimony of His loving devotion.

"Everyone told me that when I retire, I would finally have the time to do all the things I've always wanted to do. I never expected it to be so difficult to figure out what that is!" — Sharon R.

This Week's Activity

Back in Week 13, you wrote an Awaken Declaration. Now it's time to build on it with your Flourish Declaration. This is a simple two or three-sentence statement that captures how your heart has changed over the last few months. It is a milestone that shows you are moving toward the full light we have been talking about.

In your journal, start with the phrase: I used to think flourishing was... (Maybe you thought it was a high salary, a busy calendar, or being needed by everyone at work).

Then finish with: "Now I know flourishing is —" (Perhaps you've discovered it's about peace, being present, or trusting God to carry you).

Sign it and date it. Put it right next to your first declaration. You are creating a written record of how God is renewing you from the inside out. You have finished two phases of this journey; two more to go. You are halfway through a year of transformation, and the path is only getting brighter.

Optional Radiance Journal Prompts

- How has your definition of fruitfulness changed

since you started this journey?

- Olive trees are evergreen, meaning they don't lose their leaves in the winter. What is one part of your faith that has stayed green even in hard times?
- When you think about the oil being pressed from your life now, what do you think your most valuable "oil" is?

Prayer

Lord, thank You for planting me in Your house. Thank You that I don't have to be a young sapling to be useful or beautiful in Your eyes. I am grateful for the time I have had and the roots you have grown in me. Help me to trust Your loving devotion today and every day. Thank You for the fruit You are still producing in my life. In Jesus' name, Amen.

Phase Three: Strengthen – Weeks 27-39

Isaiah 40:29 · Proverbs 28:1 · 2 Timothy 1:7

Phase One was about learning who you are, and Phase Two was about learning to receive. In Phase Three, we begin to build momentum as we get stronger. Not the deadline-driven movement of your working years, but a steadier and more deliberate kind of courage. Over the next thirteen weeks, you will look honestly at the places where fear has been sitting in the driver's seat, practice setting boundaries without guilt, and discover that the boldness God offers is not the absence of uncertainty but the refusal to let uncertainty have the last word. You are not winding down. You are being wound up for something that requires exactly the kind of woman you have become.

If you haven't downloaded the Flourish Journey map by scanning the QR code:

Week 27: He Gives Strength to the Weary

When we think of Isaiah 40, we usually jump straight to the part about soaring on wings like eagles. We want strength, the ability to run without getting tired, and the feeling of lifting ourselves above our problems. But the chapter doesn't begin with eagles. It begins with exhausted people.

Isaiah is speaking to a nation that feels drained and discouraged. They believe God has forgotten them. Their strength is gone, and their future feels uncertain. Before God ever talks about soaring, He acknowledges their weariness.

Not soaring, but being tired enough to admit you need help. Most of life is lived in that third category. We are not always soaring. We are walking forward, one steady step at a time. Isaiah's message is that God strengthens people even for that quiet, ordinary progress.

"I tried to believe all my life that I couldn't ask for help from anybody else. Now that I'm older, I have no choice but to be OK with being tired and recognizing that I really can't do it on my own anymore." — Brenda K.

This Week's Activity

Part of receiving the strength God promises is recognizing where our energy goes.

Take a sheet of paper and draw two columns. Label one

"Drains My Strength" and the other "Restores My Strength." Under the first column, write the things that leave you feeling depleted: overcommitment, worry, constant bad news on TV, lack of rest, etc.

Under the second column, list the things that help restore you: time with God, sleep, a walk, a nourishing meal, dark chocolate, spending time with people you love, prayer, etc.

Then look over the list and identify ways to adjust your "restore" column.

Optional Radiance Journal Prompts

- Where do you feel like you need the most strength? Is it in your body, your thoughts, or a specific relationship?
- How does it feel to know that God acknowledges your exhaustion before He asks you to soar?
- What is one thing on your should-do list that you feel the Holy Spirit might be permitting you to let go of?

Prayer

Lord, thank You for meeting me right where I am. Thank You that I don't have to hide my tiredness from You. I hand You my weak places today and ask for Your power to fill them up. Help me to listen to the Holy Spirit as I plan my week, so I don't take on burdens You never intended for me to carry. I trust You to increase my strength just when I need it most. In Jesus' name, Amen.

"But those who wait upon the LORD will renew their strength; they will mount up with wings like eagles; they will run and not grow weary, they will walk and not faint."
Isaiah 40:31

Like last week's verse, it's worth paying attention to the order of actions in this verse. Soaring comes before running, and running comes before walking. Most of us would put it the other way around. We think we have to learn to walk first, then run, and maybe someday—if we are lucky—we will get to fly. But God doesn't start with the basics. He starts with the extraordinary.

He begins with soaring because He wants you to know that the full range of your life is available to you now. Retirement is often painted as a landing, but God calls it a launching. An eagle doesn't flap its wings constantly to stay high in the air. It finds a warm wind, and it stretches its wings out to be lifted. That is what waiting on the Lord looks like. It isn't sitting around doing nothing. It is stretching out your faith and letting His Spirit lift you higher than you could ever go on your own.

You have the wisdom to know where the warm winds of God's presence are. There is no age limit on the heights God wants to show you.

"I finally feel free from the need to please everyone but God." — Catherine D.

Look up a short video of an eagle soaring. Try to find one that has a narrator who explains what is happening. Notice how eagles soar and stay in flight without flapping their wings. Notice how they wait for the "lift" before they take off.

Optional Radiance Journal Prompts

- How does the idea of soaring before walking change how you will approach a big challenge you have in front of you?
- Isaiah 40:31 implies an exchange: waiting for the Lord leads to renewed strength. What would that look like if you waited for the Lord to lift you before you act?

Prayer

Lord, thank You for the promise that You will renew my strength. I am tired of trying to flap my wings in my own power. Today, I choose to wait on You. I stretch out my heart and ask Your Spirit to lift me. Help me to be brave enough to name the steps I've been afraid to take. Thank You for being the God who leads me into high places. I want to see the world from Your perspective today. In Jesus' name, Amen.

Week 29: Bold as a Lion

There is a very specific kind of boldness that belongs to the woman who has nothing left to prove. For years, you might have felt like you had to say yes to everything to show you were a team player, a good mom, or a hard worker. But retirement and age have a way of taking all those presumptions away. We tend to become bolder as we age.

The Bible says the righteous are as bold as a lion. A lion doesn't have to growl or pace to prove it is powerful. It is aware of its place in the world. That same boldness gives you the integrity to say no to things, without explanation, that no longer serve God's plan for you.

When we respect and fear God more than we fear people's opinions, we have more time for the things God has been nudging us toward.

"I spent my whole career worrying about what people thought of my 'no.' Now that I'm retired, I've realized that my time is a gift from God, and I don't have to apologize for how I use it." — Elena R.

This Week's Activity

The Gracious No. Retirement often makes you everyone's favorite candidate for every volunteer committee, every favor, and every errand. While your heart is generous, saying yes to everything is a recipe for exhaustion, not flourishing. A gracious no is not an act of unkindness; it is

an act of integrity.

This week, come up with your own clear, warm way to say no and practice saying it out loud until it sounds like you. People are more likely to trust a woman who means what she says, far more than a woman who says yes to everything but can only deliver on half of it.

- What is one ask or commitment you are currently saying yes to that is actually draining the strength God wants to use elsewhere?
- What is the bold move God has been nudging you toward lately? What is the one thing stopping you from starting?

Lord, thank You for the strength that comes from being Yours. I want to be as bold as a lion, because You are powerful. Help me to place my fear in You alone so that I can stop worrying about what others think. Give me the grace to say no when I need to, and the courage to say yes to the bold things You have for me. I choose to believe that I have nothing to prove and everything to enjoy in You. In Jesus' name, Amen.

Week 30: More Than Conquerors

You don't get to be a conqueror if you've never had to face a battle. In Romans 8, the apostle Paul gives us a heavy list of what those battles look like: trouble, hard times, hunger, and even danger. He says that through all of these things, we are more than conquerors.

This is not a verse about being tough or having a lot of willpower. It is a verse about what God's love can do to a life. You have lived long enough to know exactly what Paul is talking about. You have walked through seasons that felt like they might break you. You have faced losses that felt too heavy to carry. And yet, here you are.

Being more than a conqueror means that the hard things didn't just fail to destroy you; instead, they actually ended up serving you. They gave you a strength you didn't have before. They taught you that God is faithful when everything else falls away. You aren't entering retirement as a beginner; you are entering it as a veteran. You have already won the biggest battles of your life because you are still standing in His love.

*"I tell my grandchildren that real victory is the
refusal to let go of God's hand." — Miriam H.*

This Week's Activity

Pull out your free gift, the Flourish Journey Map. Write Your Conqueror's Record, looking at the evidence of God's

faithfulness in your life. Make a list of the hardest things you have already walked through. Include the losses, the health scares, or the times when you were certain you wouldn't make it to the other side. Next to each item, write one sentence about what God did or what that experience gave you.

- When you look at your Conqueror's Record, which victory surprised you the most at the time?
- Paul says we are conquerors through Him who loved us. How does knowing you are deeply loved change the way you face a new challenge?
- What is a current struggle that you can add to your list, trusting that God is already working out the victory?
- How does your past resilience give you boldness as you look at the future?

Lord, thank You that I don't have to fear the future because I have seen Your faithfulness in my past. Thank You for carrying me through the fires and the floods. I admit that sometimes I forget I am a conqueror and I start acting like a victim. Help me remember my record this week. Let Your love be the source of my strength so I can face every new day with a bold and steady heart. In Jesus' name, Amen.

Week 31: Spirit of Power, Love, and Self-Discipline

Fear is a spirit, according to 2 Timothy 1:7. You weren't born a worrier, or to carry anxiety as a permanent part of your retirement. What God actually placed inside you is a powerful triad: power, love, and self-control. These three qualities cover everything you need to step boldly into whatever is next. Power gives you the strength to act. Love gives you the heart to serve. Self-control gives you the steady mind to make wise choices without being tossed around by your emotions.

Take a clear-eyed look at your life. Where are power, love, and self-control flowing freely? And where has fear been sitting in the driver's seat? We aren't looking for these things to produce guilt. We are looking for them so we can identify the specific places where God is ready to do a replacement. If a thought or a habit didn't come from Him, you have full permission to hand it back. If it did come from Him, you have every right to walk in it with your head held high.

> "Worrying has always been part of my default reaction. Almost like a responsibility. But worry doesn't make a good testimony. So, I'm learning to trust Him with my petty problems so I can show the world that I am calm and at peace." — Martha H.

This Week's Activity

Try a News Fast. The daily news cycle feeds are counting on you to stay tuned, while they raise our adrenaline with sensational, negative stories designed to keep us captive. We don't need to know everything that is going on in the world. A lot of what the media tells us is urgent isn't. Just see if you can try a total news fast. For seven days, don't check the headlines, turn off the news channels, and unsubscribe from social media accounts that leave you feeling anxious or depleted.

Optional Radiance Journal Prompts

- When you think of the word power, how does it apply to your life as a retired woman of faith?
- Which of the three words, power, love, or self-control, do you feel most strongly in your life? The weakest?
- How did your first day of the news fast change the way you felt in your spirit?

Prayer

Lord, thank You that You haven't left me to struggle with fear on my own. I hand back the anxiety and the what-ifs that have been weighing me down. I choose to receive the power, love, and self-control You have already placed in me. Help me guard my mind this week and focus on Your goodness rather than the world's problems. I want to walk in the boldness that comes from Your Spirit alone. In Jesus' name, Amen.

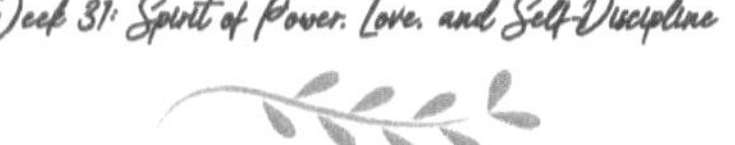

"But He said to me, 'My grace is sufficient for you, for My power is perfected in weakness.' Therefore I will boast all the more gladly in my weaknesses, so that the power of Christ may rest on me." 2 Corinthians 12:9

Paul was not writing these words from comfort. In the same chapter, he describes a "thorn in the flesh," a painful, persistent condition he asked God to remove three times. Instead of taking the thorn away, God gave him an understanding of how His grace works.

He was showing him that human strength eventually reaches its limit. There comes a point when effort, talent, and determination can no longer carry us forward. At that point, we discover something Paul had to learn himself: the outcome has always been in God's hands.

Instead of removing the thorn, God revealed that the limitation itself would become the place where divine strength was most visible.

That is why Paul says he would "boast" in his weaknesses. He is not celebrating pain or playing the martyr. He is recognizing that the moments when he can no longer rely on himself are the very moments when Christ's sustaining power becomes most evident.

As we age, our physical limitations, emotional transitions, and changing roles can make us feel less capable than we once were. But those changes often open the door to a richer kind of trust. Instead of measuring life by productivity or constant activity, we begin to see how God continues to work through us in powerful ways. When we reach the limits of

our own strength, we are often standing in the very place where His strength becomes most clear.

The grace that sustained Paul in his weakness is the same grace you now carry for others — you pray with authority not because you have it together, but because you have learned where the strength actually comes from.

"God's grace is free and requires no payment. Accepting that sometimes requires a special kind of surrender that isn't always easy for us." — Sarah M.

This Week's Activity

Specifically pray for someone else. Start looking for opportunities to become an intercessor for others. Pray with the posture of Mark 11:24. Ask as if you already trust that God has heard you and is already at work. Record it in your journal and leave room for you to note when the prayer was answered.

Optional Radiance Journal Prompts

- Paul found that God's power was perfected in his thorn. What limitation or weakness in your life feels like a thorn?
- How does it change your perspective to think of your limitations as the address where grace takes up residence?
- Where have you seen God's strength show up in your life after your own resources were completely exhausted?
- If you stopped trying to produce results this week, what kind of internal depth could God cultivate in

you instead?

Lord, thank You that Your grace is not a backup plan. It is the main event. Forgive me for the times I have reached for my own resources first and treated You like a last resort. I come to You now knowing that where I am limited, You are not. I pray today for _____________________, and I ask this not with a whisper but with the full confidence of a daughter who knows her Father hears her. Do what only You can do. I will wait faithfully for You to move how You see fit. In Jesus' name, Amen.

> *"Do not fear, for I am with you; do not be afraid, for I am your God. I will strengthen you; I will surely help you; I will uphold you with My righteous right hand." Isaiah 41:10*

The verse holds five specific promises:

- I am with you.
- I am your God.
- I will strengthen.
- I will surely help.
- I will uphold.

Not one comes with a condition. Each statement moves closer and becomes more personal. First comes presence: I am with you. Then, the relationship: I am your God. After that comes the actions God Himself promises to take: strengthening, helping, and upholding.

None of these promises is tied to your performance. God does not say, "If you are strong enough," or "If you manage your fears well." The foundation of every promise is who He is.

Fear loses its power not because we suddenly become fearless, but because God places His presence, His help, and His strength underneath us.

> *"I used to think being brave meant I didn't feel the butterflies in my stomach. Now I realize bravery is*

just holding God's hand while the butterflies are flying." — Martha T.

This Week's Activity

When something goes sideways, and yes, it will, try to make your first response be this one question: "I wonder how God is going to work this out." And say it with a playful, expectant attitude. You're not denying reality; you're accepting God at his word. Place your faith in God's track record so far. Meet each new obstacle with genuine curiosity about what your Heavenly Father is working through in your life. This kind of joy is not naive. It is the most mature response available to someone who knows exactly who is in charge of her life.

Optional Radiance Journal Prompts

- Which of the five promises in Isaiah 41:10 brings you the most comfort and why?
- What is one specific fear about your future that you have been trying to handle on your own?
- Think back to a time in your past when an obstacle turned into a blessing. How did God uphold you during that transition?
- When you tell yourself, I wonder how God is going to work this out, how does the physical tension in your body change?

Prayer

Lord, thank You that I am never alone, even when the house is quiet or when I am not sure if things can work out for good. I'm handing You my fears of being forgotten and

becoming irrelevant. I choose to believe that You are my God and that You are holding me steady with Your righteous hand. Help me face every hiccup this week with a heart full of curiosity rather than worry. I trust Your record because You have never failed me yet. I can't wait to see how You will help me today. In Jesus' name, Amen.

Week 34: Be Strong and Courageous

God told Joshua to be strong and courageous before he had even dipped a toe in the Jordan River. He said it before the walls fell and before a single piece of evidence confirmed that God's command was even possible. Our Heavenly Father knows us well; we need courage first. But how many times do we ask him for it?

God will call us to new territory before we can see what is waiting there. He does this because He knows that if we could see the obstacles and "lessons" we'd need to learn along the way, we would turn around, full stop, and not move.

God never gives us a perfect strategy. But He will give you courage to face whatever is in front of you, and He will hold your hand every step of the way. And along the way, He will use every step to teach you.

You might think retirement is the time to retreat and play it safe. But you can be sure that God still has some adventures in store for you. The same God who was with you in the boardroom, the classroom, or the factory floor is with you in this new space. You are moving forward under His command, and that is the most secure position you can ever be in.

*"I spent forty years working out schedules and plans.
It's been a challenge learning how to "free fall"
through my days. But one thing that is non-negotiable*

for me is spending time with Jesus every morning."
— Janet R.

This Week's Activity

Write your commission this week. Write a paragraph to yourself from the perspective of God, who has been with you every single mile of your journey so far.

Write what He would say to you about the territory ahead; something rooted in biblical promises and truths?

What does He know about your character that makes Him completely certain you are ready for this? What is He still teaching you?

Sign it and date it, put it in an envelope beside your bed, with a date to open it one year from today.

Optional Radiance Journal Prompts

- Joshua had to leave the desert to enter the Promised Land. What "desert habit" or old way of thinking do you need to leave behind to move into your new territory?
- When you hear the words be strong and courageous, does it feel like a gift of permission?
- What is one thing you feel drawn toward doing that requires you to trust God more than your own experience?
- How does the promise that God is with you wherever you go change how you feel about your schedule this week?

Lord, thank You that You never ask me to go anywhere that You haven't already been. I confess that I sometimes wait for a sign before I am willing to be brave. Today, I choose to be courageous because You commanded it. I am stepping into this new territory with my head held high, knowing You are right beside me. Thank You for preparing the way and for seeing the strength in me that I sometimes forget I have. I am ready for the adventure. In Jesus' name, Amen.

"Be kind and tenderhearted to one another, forgiving each other just as in Christ God forgave you." Ephesians 4:32

Being busy and managing a household can be a great distraction from what is really going on in our hearts. When we're consumed by work, racing to events, and keeping up with daily demands, it's easy to ignore that nagging feeling of resentment. But now that the pace has changed, those memories can start to knock on the door, and you might find old ones coming up. Old family rifts, work relationships that ended badly, and especially those things you said that you wish you could take back. And now it's too late.

Ephesians 4:32 doesn't require a permission slip from the other person. It doesn't demand that we wait until the other person deserves our kindness or until they come to us with a sincere apology. It says you can start the forgiveness process – immediately, and peace will follow. But we know, it's not that simple.

R.T. Kendall, in *Total Forgiveness*, says forgiveness is not a feeling that arrives when you are ready, but as a decision you make before you feel like making it. And it's about trust; trusting to release the entire situation, the person, into God's hands entirely, and walking away free from the burden of what happened. Trying to forgive without releasing the burden of it to God is exhausting and impossible. Kendall emphasizes Ephesians 4:32 when he says it is a conscious choice that you make before you or the other person deserves it.

Note that self-forgiveness belongs in this same sentence. We often find it easier to believe God can forgive the whole world than to believe He can forgive our own past mistakes. And even harder for us to forgive ourselves. But His grace was never meant to extend to everyone except you. Holding onto shame doesn't make you more holy; it just makes you more tired.

"For years, I blamed my resentment on my hectic work schedule that never gave me a chance to relax. So, when I retired, the peace and freedom I expected still didn't come. And this was because the grudge I'd been carrying for years wasn't going away on its own. I had to do my part by releasing this into God's hands and by starting to forgive the people I thought didn't deserve my forgiveness." — Brenda L.

This Week's Activity

Pick up your journal and just write down everything about one event you cannot let go of. Write uncensored, knowing you are going to throw (or burn) this when you're done. Record every hurt; every justification on why you deserve to be so angry, and what the other person should do to make it right for you. Keep going until you've covered every last drop of the pain. This might take several sessions. When you've felt physically spent, write another prayer, asking the Holy Spirit to soften your heart, give you compassion, and grant you the power to forgive. Start by forgiving yourself for carrying the hurt so long. Peace may not arrive instantly. But you do have to make the choice. Let God reveal to you if you need to have a conversation with someone else; ask God to give you the courage and the right moment to speak.

Optional Radiance Journal Prompts

- What old memories or grudges have started to come to mind more often?
- What does it mean to you personally to be tenderhearted toward yourself regarding your past mistakes?
- How would your daily life feel different if you were no longer carrying the weight of that one specific resentment?
- Looking at Ephesians 4:32, how does remembering God's forgiveness toward you make it easier to extend that same grace to someone who hurt you?

Prayer

Lord, thank You that Your grace is bigger than my past and stronger than my regrets. I admit that I have been holding onto some things that are far too heavy for me. Today, I name ___________________ and I choose to release them and the situation into Your hands. Please soften my heart, which has grown hard, and give me the courage to forgive myself, too. I want to live this new chapter of my life with a light heart and a clear mind. Help me to be kind and tenderhearted, just as You are with me. In Jesus' name, Amen.

Week 36: Restore What the Locusts Have Taken

"I will repay you for the years eaten by locusts." Joel 2:25

The promise in Joel 2:25 is familiar, but its essence is that, in one of the most overlooked parts of the restoration, God first acknowledges the damage. The locusts came. The crops were consumed. God is graciously saying that He sees what happened, and He honors it. He doesn't ask you to minimize the years that were lost to grief, the wrong turns you took, or the years you spent just surviving instead of really living because of an illness. He names the loss. He sees the damage. And then He says He will restore it.

Notice that the verse uses the word restore or repay instead of replace. This means He can take what was taken and give you back something more whole than you had before. Throughout the stories in the Bible, God repeatedly provides proof that He does restore:

Job: After Job had prayed for his friends, the LORD restored his prosperity and gave him twice as much as he had before. (Job 42:10). So the LORD blessed the latter part of Job's life more than his first. He had 14,000 sheep, 6,000 camels, 1,000 yoke of oxen, and 1,000 female donkeys. (Job 42:12).

Joseph: After being thrown in a pit, losing his family, his freedom, and his reputation, Joseph rises to leadership in Egypt and is in charge of the whole land of Egypt, riding in a chariot. (Genesis 41:41-43).

Ruth: After being widowed, losing both sons, and being

virtually homeless, Ruth becomes the great-grandmother of David. (Ruth 4:14-15).

Joel 2:25 doesn't promise to rewind time. It promises that what was consumed will not have the final word. In Scripture, restoration means that God reclaims what seemed wasted and integrates it into a greater story. God is the master of turning a field that looks bare into a green, thriving one again. The calendar doesn't limit him. He can pack more joy, more purpose, and more life into your later years than you had in all the years the locusts were busy.

The swarming locusts of the past do not get the final word on your legacy. God has a way of making the second half of the story so rich that the earlier losses begin to look like a backdrop for something you could have never planned. Trust Him to do the work of mending. He is a very kind and efficient Gardener.

> *"I have always believed in continuing to learn. I read a LOT, not just novels but also creative nonfiction, history, and informative works. It grieves me that reading is becoming a dying art. One should never stop expanding one's mind or rejoicing in things previously not known! This is my habit." — Carmen R.*

This Week's Activity

God works quietly, mysteriously, and sometimes imperceptibly. You likely have restoration stories that you've overlooked. Make a list of things you thought were hopeless that have somehow resolved into something better. Thank God for what He's already done for you, and for what

He's about to do.

- How does it change your thoughts about the past hurts when you think about how God restores and acknowledges what you've been through?
- In what ways can you see God bringing green back into areas of your life that felt bare just a few years ago?
- Is there still an area where you're waiting for God's restoration?

Lord, thank You that You are the Great Restorer. I hand You the years that feel eaten away by stress, regret, and things I cannot change. I choose to believe Your promise in Joel 2:25 today. I am asking You to do a deep work in my heart and my life, bringing beauty out of the places that felt wasted. Thank You that my best days are defined by Your grace and not by my past losses. I am holding my hands open to receive the restoration You have planned. In Jesus' name, Amen.

Week 37: The Roles That Remain

"Older women, likewise, are to be reverent in their behavior, not slanderers or addicted to much wine, but teachers of good." Titus 2:3

There will be an unspoken renegotiation within your family and social circles that occurs almost immediately upon your retirement. This shift is the inverse of your working years, when everyone needed access to you. For example, you may have been the spot everyone comes to for Thanksgiving. And then, everything starts to change.

Change is inevitable, and if you think any of the changes suggest you are fading, Titus 2:3 is a reminder of how valuable your role is now, in many different ways. The verse describes women with years of experience as having a vital, specific function: to teach what is good.

If you have children, you've already experienced how they have come to need you less in immediate, practical ways, such as rides to school, meals, comfort in the middle of the night, and help with decisions. You can count on this dependence to continue changing as they marry and you become a smaller part of their growing, expanding lives. That awareness can sometimes sting, and it carries its own form of grief.

Scripture encourages this independence. "For each one should carry his own load" (Galatians 6:5). But alongside this, Titus 2:3 becomes especially meaningful. You are still shaping lives by sharing the understanding and wisdom God is still building in you.

Yet, while it does evolve, you can ensure your influence doesn't disappear. Let the wisdom God has blessed you with be a treasure to others. Guidance is most powerful when it is offered with humility rather than control. "Let your gentleness be apparent to all" (Philippians 4:5). Wisdom pressed too hard is often resisted.

The goal is certainly not about micro-managing everyone else's lives, but to walk beside them as a steady witness to God's faithfulness. Titus describes older women as "teachers of what is good" whose lives encourage others toward wisdom (Titus 2:3–4). The influence comes from our character: reverence, steadiness, and a life that reflects God's faithfulness over time.

As Proverbs 16:21 says, "The wise in heart are called discerning, and pleasant speech increases learning." Wisdom offered with humility has a way of traveling farther than advice forced into someone's hands. Your role is to support and to help make the road clearer.

When wisdom is offered with grace, it becomes something others want to draw from rather than something they feel they are being pushed to accept.

Ensure your influence doesn't end. You are moving from a role defined by what you did to one now defined by who you are and what you share with the world. This is a high calling. You are the keeper of the stories and the witness of God's faithfulness. When you share what you know, you aren't just talking about the past; you are building a bridge for someone else to walk on. Your influence continues through the beautiful authority of a life that has walked the road with Jesus for many years.

"The way you've overcome setbacks can be a guide to someone else; don't hide the landmarks God helped you build." — Sue W.

This Week's Activity

At the top of a journal page, write this heading: What I've learned that I wish I knew then. This is likely impossible to do in one sitting. But collect your wisdom and organize it. Then, ask God to bring people and circumstances in your life that allow you to help someone else by sharing what He's taught you.

Optional Radiance Journal Prompts

- Which of your old work roles has been the hardest to let go of, and why?
- When you look at the younger women in your circle, what is one struggle they face that you feel uniquely equipped to speak into?
- Titus 2:3 mentions being reverent in behavior. What does a life of reverence look like to you in this current stage?
- How does it feel to think of yourself as a teacher of what is good rather than someone who is finished with their career?

Prayer

Lord, thank You that my purpose doesn't have an expiration date. Forgive me for the times I have felt like my best contributions were behind me. Open my eyes to the women around me who are walking paths I have already traveled.

Give me the right words and the right timing to teach what is good. Help me to give from my overflow and to see my gray hair as the crown of wisdom You say it is. Use my life to encourage someone else today. In Jesus' name, Amen.

"Do not grieve, for the joy of the LORD is your strength."
Nehemiah 8:10

The words in Nehemiah 8:10 were spoken to the people who were crying because they had just heard the Law read aloud and suddenly realized how far they had drifted from God. They were weeping because of conviction and guilt.

After showing them the gap, they were told to stop mourning and start celebrating. They were instructed to go home, share food, and mark the day as holy. After recognizing the gap, the next step is joy.

Imagine having that advice handed down to you from the "powers that be" at your last job. At work, when a problem is uncovered, most leaders demand more effort, more pressure, or more correction. In this case, God prescribed something different. Joy.

Seen through the lens of this verse, joy becomes a kind of secret weapon. More than a fleeting good mood or a bubbly emotion that rises and falls with circumstances. It is the steady confidence that God is still at work. When you are free from guilt, drudgery, and sorrow, *you* have the energy to keep going the extra mile.

"I tell my newly retired friends to first enjoy your
newfound downtime. Then start thinking about these
golden years as putting "you" in the new life, and
take care of some of your needs.... God, health,

*physical appearance and whatever else brings them
joy." — Pam S.*

This Week's Activity

Follow the advice in Nehemiah 8:10. "Go and eat what is rich, drink what is sweet, and send portions to those who have nothing prepared…", invite friends or family, and host a celebration. You don't have to have a reason to do this, other than to celebrate all that God has done in your life.

Optional Radiance Journal Prompts

- When was the last time you felt undone by God's kindness toward you?
- How do you distinguish between manufactured cheerfulness and the deep, settled joy mentioned in Nehemiah?
- How would your physical energy change this week if you truly believed God was genuinely proud of you and wanted you to eat what is rich, drink something sweet, and enjoy your birthright?

Prayer

Lord, thank You that Your joy is not something I have to stir up on my own. I confess that I sometimes try to rely on my own grit instead of Your grace. Today, I choose to rest in the joy of knowing I am Yours. Thank You for being the foundation that holds me up when I feel weak. I pray for ___________________________, asking that they would feel this same spiritual joy today. I am watching for the ways You will delight me this week. In Jesus' name, Amen.

Week 39: Strengthen: Phase Three Reflection

We have reached the end of Phase Three. For thirteen weeks, the work has been about throwing things off — fear, old measurements of worth, the habit of filling every silence with noise, the weight of old hurts that were never yours to carry forever. Hebrews 12:1 names that work exactly: throw off every encumbrance. You have been doing that. And now, lighter than you were, you are being commissioned to run.

The verse doesn't say run fast. It says run with endurance, which is a different thing entirely. Speed is what you needed during your career years. Endurance defines this chapter of your life. The woman who finishes well isn't the one who sprinted the first mile; she's the one who was still moving when the road got long and unmarked, and no one was watching.

Hebrews 12:1 arrives on the heels of an entire chapter, the Hall of Faith that names the women and men who ran before you. Sarah. Rahab. The unnamed ones who went about in sheepskins and goatskins and never saw the promise fulfilled in their lifetime but kept going anyway. They are the cloud of witnesses. They didn't get the completed promise in their lifetimes. You may not see all of yours either. But they kept running — and that is exactly the testimony their

lives are sending forward to you today. Their road was not easy; their stories are recorded precisely because they weren't. Sarah waited decades for a promise that seemed impossible. Rahab risked everything on a God she had only heard about. Others endured hardship, loss, and uncertainty without ever seeing the full outcome of their beliefs. Scripture doesn't sugarcoat those struggles. It reveals them.

Hebrews says they are a "cloud of witnesses," which means their lives stand as testimony. They are evidence that faith can endure through long stretches of uncertainty. Their stories remind us that the race of faith has always been run by ordinary people who kept moving forward when the road looked unclear.

Endurance is more than dramatic bursts of effort; it is steady steps taken over time. One faithful choice. One act of trust. One more mile walked with God. And you're already in the race.

"True strength is letting go and being willing to let Him carry it for me." — Sandra P.

Write your Strength Declaration this week. This short testimony paragraph helps you see how far you have come.

- Looking back at the last thirteen weeks, what is one fight or struggle that you can say you have fought well with God's help?
- The writer of Hebrews names two things to throw

off: encumbrances and sin. Which of these — an encumbrance or a specific sin — has been the heavier weight for you this phase?

- What is one thing you used to worry about every morning that no longer holds power over your day?
- As you move into the final phase of this year, what course do you feel God is calling you to finish with joy?

Prayer

Lord, thank You for the strength You have built in me over these last few months. I praise You because I am not the same woman I was thirteen weeks ago. Thank You for carrying me when I was tired and for teaching me that Your grace is all I really need. I am stepping into this next phase with my eyes on You, ready to see the fruit You are growing in my life. In Jesus' name, Amen.

Phase Four: Fruitful — Weeks 40-52

Everything you have walked through this year has been preparation for this. The awakening, the daily renewal, the hard work of building courage — all of it has been growing something in you that is now ready to be given away. Phase Four is about the harvest: the stories you carry, the wisdom you have earned, the prayers only you have been praying for the people you love. Psalm 71:18 gives you your assignment plainly — declare God's power to the next generation. You are not finished. You are not fading. You are standing in the full light of a life that was always heading somewhere worth arriving at, and the fruit you bear now will outlast everything that came before it.

If you haven't downloaded the Flourish Journey map by scanning the QR code:

Week 40: God's Handiwork

We are returning to the verse that opened this devotional, but you are no longer the same woman who read these words back in Week 1. When you read the word workmanship, or masterpiece, as some translations put it, I hope you are seeing it with entirely new eyes. This isn't just a nice idea about your potential anymore. It is a duty to accept this as reality. You are the intentional, deliberate, and glorious work of a God who knew exactly what He was making before He ever drew the first breath into your lungs.

It would make sense for you to tie your job description to your career and work. Value, in the worldly view, is always tied to our production. But don't you have talents, gifts, and skills that were never part of your career? God put them there for you to use and to bring you joy.

You were created for good works that God prepared in advance. Notice that the verse says He prepared them for us, so that we could walk in them. You don't have to stress about inventing a new purpose for your retirement. You just have to look for the path He already paved. He isn't finished with His masterpiece yet; He is just starting a beautiful new chapter of the story.

"I like to tell myself that I was a masterpiece before I ever clocked in for my first shift. The work didn't make me; God did." — Beverly W.

This week, create what you might call a Masterpiece Map.

Take a large sheet of paper or open a two-page spread in your journal. Write your name in the center. From there, begin mapping the qualities, gifts, and patterns you now recognize as part of your design. You can make it as creative as you like—colored pencils, markers, watercolor—or keep it simple with a pencil and a notepad.

Start by noticing what skills, talents, and activities keep showing up. What kinds of things do people naturally volunteer you for? What about these things seems to drain you, versus what gives you joy? See if you can differentiate what makes you different. It doesn't have to be a specific activity – maybe you have a gift for listening and helping people figure out what to do next. Or maybe you dread hosting, but love to bake. Write these around your name and draw connections between the ones that seem related.

When you step back and look at the page, you may start to see a pattern you had never thought of before. What once felt like scattered abilities now looks more like intentional design.

Start to think about ways you would like to expand on those things that bring you joy, and say no to those that don't. And if there is something you're particularly drawn to, think about taking a class or joining a group that will help you develop those skills even more.

Optional Radiance Journal Prompts

- When you read the word masterpiece today, how

does your heart respond differently than it did at the beginning of the year?

- Looking at your Masterpiece Map, which gift or quality surprised you the most when you saw it on paper?
- How does it feel to know that your value is based on being God's workmanship rather than your own hard work?

Prayer

Lord, thank You for the way You have shaped my life with such detail and love. I praise You because I am Your workmanship, created with a purpose that goes far beyond any job I've ever held. Help me to see myself the way You see me as a masterpiece in progress. Lead me into the good works You have already prepared for me today. I am ready to walk in them. In Jesus' name, Amen.

Week 41: The Plans I Have For You

We see Jeremiah 29:11 on coffee mugs and graduation cards. We treat it like a sunny promise for people just starting. But these words were originally written to people in exile. They weren't sitting at the foot of a mountain waiting for their lives to start, with no regrets or mistakes behind them. They were sitting in the rubble of what used to be their lives, wondering if God had checked out on them completely.

That makes this the perfect verse for this exact moment in your story. You might be sitting in the rubble of a long career, broken relationships, and wondering what these wide-open days are actually for. When the structure of a forty-hour work week disappears, the verse takes on a whole new meaning. But the voice is as true for you today as it was in your 20s. He is still the Architect of your days.

The plans He has for you did not end when your career did. In fact, some of His most beautiful designs are only becoming possible now because you finally have the time and the freedom to walk in them.

These open days are a gift to be unwrapped. Don't think He's looking at your retirement as a winding down, but as a scaling up of your heart's influence. You have been given the great gift of time, and God has specific, joyful plans for how you will spend it.

"I quoted Jeremiah 29 so many times to my kids while they were growing up that they already had it memorized before they left home. I never realized it was meant for me at sixty-five, too. God didn't stop having plans for me just because my office no longer had a desk." — Martha S.

This Week's Activity

Make a Jar of Adventures. Write down everything you have always wanted to do but haven't yet; include small things like trying a new cafe, to bigger things like taking an art class, visiting a state park you've never seen, or a big vacation. Cut them up individually and put them in a jar.

Next, pull out three slips and put them on your calendar: one for this month, one for next month, and one for the next. A dream that stays on a slip of paper is just a wish, but a dream that lands on a calendar becomes a beginning. Start making plans; decide who you're going to invite and make them happen.

Optional Radiance Journal Prompts

- When you were twenty years old, what did you think your future would look like at this age? How is God's plan better?
- Why is it sometimes harder to trust God with our open days than it was to trust Him with our busy work days?

Prayer

Lord, thank You that You are not finished with me. Forgive

me for thinking that my best plans were tied to my paycheck. I choose to believe that You have a hope and a future prepared for me that is even better than my past. I hand You my calendar and my open days, asking You to lead me into the adventures You have planned. I am excited to see what You are unfolding for me. In Jesus' name, Amen.

Week 42: The Crown You've Earned

> *"Gray hair is a crown of glory; it is attained along the path of righteousness." Proverbs 16:31*

This chapter is not about cancelling your appointment at the hair salon. It's more about becoming proud of the changes that are happening within us. Why do we treat those silver strands like uninvited guests at a party? Likely, it's because society has conditioned us to believe that youth is the goal. We can still color our grays if we want: what's important here is the mindset shift. What if we really did view our gray hairs as crowns?

A few weeks ago, back in Week 37, we looked at how our roles in our families and the world change after we retire. We talked about becoming a teacher of what is good. This week is a beautiful companion to that truth, but it goes a step further into who you are. While Week 37 was about the work of sharing wisdom, Week 42 is about the honor of the life you have lived. This isn't just about what you do; it is about the glory God sees when He looks at you.

In the Bible, a crown is a symbol of victory. You have earned every single gray hair. You may have earned them by worrying over your finances or your children, by the time you spent building a career, and by the many nights you leaned on God when life felt impossible. Every silver hair is a marker of a prayer God answered, a trial you survived, and a mile you walked in faith. It is the visual proof that God has been faithful to you for a very long time.

In her book, *Choosing Gratitude: Your Journey to Joy,*

Nancy DeMoss Wolgemuth shares a story about a woman who had spent over fifty years memorizing scripture. This woman didn't view her age as a loss. Instead, she used the treasure she had gathered over those fifty years to stay steady. When she felt discouraged, she would start quoting the Bible to herself, and those words would pull her back into the truth. She didn't have to go looking for strength because she had been storing it up her entire life. Her silver hair was the crown of a woman who knew exactly where her help came from.

When you see yourself in the mirror, try to see what God sees. He doesn't see someone who is fading. He sees a queen wearing a crown of glory. That crown gives you a special kind of authority in the lives of the people around you. When a younger woman sees your crown, she should see hope. Let the world see your radiance because you aren't afraid to let yourself glow from the inside.

You are not past your prime. You are standing in the full light of a life well-lived. Your gray hair is not a sign that you are finished; it is the official garment of a woman who has much to give, much to say, and a crown that shines with the goodness of God.

> *"I remember, as a child, seeing the pretty ladies in my church with their silver hair all done up in a bun on top of their heads. I thought they were so beautiful that they must be angels. I don't know why we are so quick to hide what can actually be beautiful." — Lisa M.*

This Week's Activity

Pick a verse to memorize it this week. You can pick Proverbs

16:31, your "Life Verse" from Week 9, or a verse that has comforted you while reading this book. Write it on a card in large, clear letters. Place it on your mirror so it is the first thing you see when you look at your reflection. Say it out loud every morning until you have it memorized. Memorizing it ensures it stays with you, so you can easily reach for it in your mind when you need it.

- When you look in the mirror, do you usually see a crown of glory or something that needs to be hidden? How does God's view change your perspective?
- What is one mile on your path of righteousness that was particularly hard to walk, but showed you God's strength?
- How can you use the authority of your experience to encourage a younger woman who is just starting her path?

Lord, thank You for the gift of long life. Help me to see my gray hair the way You do, as a crown of glory and a sign of Your faithfulness. Forgive me for the times I have tried to hide my age rather than honor the path You have led me on. Thank You for every hard year and every joyful day that brought me to this place. Give me the grace to wear my crown with joy and to use my story to give hope to those coming behind me. In Jesus' name, Amen.

Week 43: We Will Tell

Stories are the gold of a life well-lived. In business, we often talk about currency, budgets, and bottom lines. But as you step into this new space, you realize that the most valuable thing you own isn't in a bank account. It is your collection of stories. Psalm 78:4 makes our job very clear: we will not hide them.

Last week, we focused on your identity; that silver crown of glory that marks you as a woman of experience and honor. This week, we move from the crown to the conversation. If your gray hair is the sign of the path you've walked, your stories are the map you leave behind for others. The things God has done in your life — those specific, one-of-a-kind moments that belong only to you — were never meant to be kept in a vault. Keeping them to yourself is like finding a well in a desert and refusing to tell anyone where the water is.

Think about the people coming behind you. It might be your children and your grandchildren, but it could just as easily be a relative or a young person who is close to you. Each one needs proof that God is real and that He actually cares about the details of a human life. When you share a bullet point version of your faith—saying things like, "God is good" or "He always provides"—it is true, but doesn't paint the full picture. A story is memorable and allows you to show all the turning points and "just then" moments when God turned everything around.

In his book, *When Your World Falls Apart*, David Jeremiah writes that our past experiences with God are not just memories; they are the bedrock of our future. He explains that when we face new trials, we can look back at the monuments of God's faithfulness from years ago. These stories prove that the God who rescued us then is the same God who is with us now. By telling these stories, you aren't just reminiscing. You are giving the next generation the evidence they need to trust Him when their own worlds feel like they are falling apart. They need to hear what God actually did, in plain, simple language, from someone who was there.

Don't let your memories gather dust. Your stories are the bridge that will help someone else cross over from fear into faith.

"My mother kept a journal for most of her life. She recorded things like her favorite verses, her prayers for others, and even the meals she sometimes cooked. When she died, I took them home with me. These journals are some of my most prized possessions." —
Jean L.

There is probably a story in there that you need to write down. The one that still brings you tears whenever you think about how God carried you. Don't just write the summary; write it with real detail. Where were you? What did the room feel like? What were you afraid of at that moment? It helps, when you write, to think of one person that you are telling this story to. You don't have to share it with anyone just yet; just writing it down on paper puts it on your heart so that

you're ready to share it when God provides the opportunity.

- Why do you think we sometimes hesitate to share our specific stories and instead stick to general spiritual talk?
- When you think about your life, what is the one story that still makes your heart beat a little faster because God's hand was so obvious?
- Who is one person in the generation to come who needs to hear a story of God's strength this week?
- How does remembering your own stories of God's power change the way you feel about the open days of your retirement?

Lord, thank You for being the Author of my life. Thank You for every chapter, even the ones that were hard. I ask You to bring to my mind the specific moments where You showed Your power and Your wonders. Forgive me for keeping these treasures to myself. Give me the courage to share them with those who come behind me. Help me to speak with joy and clarity so that they might put their trust in You, too. In Jesus' name, Amen.

Week 44: The Reveal

Back in Week 6, you were just beginning to look for the hidden thread. You were still in the early weeks of learning to see your life from the outside. The pattern was there, but the view was partial.

Now it is Week 44. You have been at this for nearly a year. You have moved through four phases of this journey, done the hard work of waking up to your identity, traced the morning dew of God's daily faithfulness, and built real courage in your bones. From where you are standing now, the view is different.

Romans 8:28 is one of those verses that is easy to quote and genuinely hard to live. All things work together for good, including the thing that broke your heart at forty-three, the opportunity that went to someone else, the years that felt invisible, the chapter you would erase if you could. All of it. Together. For good.

The tapestry metaphor from Week 6 is a good one to revisit. You've heard the scrambled thread story before, when all you see are knots and crossed threads and colors that don't seem to belong together. Turn it over, and the picture is there; complete, intentional, beautiful in a way that only becomes visible once enough of the work is done.

The doors that slammed shut have become *thank God*

moments in hindsight. The role that felt like a mismatch was the exact training ground for the woman you needed to become. The loss that still stings made room for something you couldn't have held alongside it. God uses everything. He is the most careful Weaver there is.

Take time going through the reveal. Your life has been intentional from the beginning; the hard chapters were not accidents; you are not a collection of random events. You are evidence of Romans 8:28.

> *"There is a version of retirement that looks like a long exhale. Finally, finally, the pressure is off. And there is real peace in that exhale. Take it. But what comes after the exhale is the interesting part: the slow work of figuring out who you are when you aren't carrying that label anymore." — Roslyn F.*

This Week's Activity

Go back to the life-milestone list you made in Week 6 and add to it everything that has happened since. Look at the whole arc. Where do you now see a thread that you couldn't see in Week 6? What has become clearer from this vantage point?

Then, look for physical clutter in your home. Clear some of it this week. Making space in your home is a physical way of honoring the Reveal. What you are becoming doesn't need to be burdened with relics of your past.

Optional Radiance Journal Prompts

- What is one tangled thread from your past that you can now see God using for good?

- What closed door in your history turned out to be God's protection rather than His rejection?
- Is there a thread you are still waiting to understand? Can you trust the Weaver with it today?

Prayer

Lord, I am amazed at how You wove the hard parts of my life into something beautiful. Forgive me for calling it "chaos" when it was actually "craftsmanship." Thank You for the promise that all things work together for good — not some things, not the easy things, all things. I trust You with the threads that still don't make sense. I love the story You are writing. In Jesus' name, Amen.

> *"For You formed my inmost being; You knit me together in my mother's womb." Psalm 139:13*

Last week was the mountaintop. You stepped back far enough to see the full tapestry, the whole arc of God's intentional leading through a life that only looked random from the inside. Romans 8:28 gave you a wide view.

Psalm 139:13 is a verse about the individual threads. God formed your inner being; the interior, the part no one else sees. He knit you together, one stitch at a time, in a place no human eye could see.

The threads that felt off-color while you were living them have helped create you. The years you spent as a caregiver that felt like a detour from your real life wove a depth of compassion into you that no shortcut could have produced, and the years you felt invisible, where you worked faithfully, and no one seemed to notice, added a layer of rooted strength. Even the threads you wish weren't there — the grief, the years when you felt stuck — were placed by hands that knew the finished pattern and needed exactly that color in exactly that place.

The difference between Week 44 and this week is the difference between seeing the whole tapestry and touching the individual threads. Both are important parts to see in light of your past. The wide view gives you faith for the future. The close view gives you gratitude for the specific, the particular, the unrepeatable details of a life that God has been attending to since before you drew your first breath.

"Make yourself look pretty even if you have nowhere to go." — Elizabeth M.

This Week's Activity

Write a short gratitude letter to one chapter of your life that you thought was hard. Write it as the woman who can now see some of the good that God was giving her. What did it actually add to who you are?

Optional Radiance Journal Prompts

- Make a list of times in your life when you didn't get what you wanted, and in hindsight turned out to be the best thing that could have happened.
- How would your life have turned out differently if you had gotten what you wished for?

Prayer

Lord, thank You for the care You have given me since the moment I was created. Thank You for the threads I would have pulled out if You had let me. They are in the pattern for a reason, and I trust the hands that placed them. In Jesus' name, Amen.

> *"You did not choose Me, but I chose you. And I appointed you to go and bear fruit—fruit that will remain." John 15:16*

Appointed. That is a heavy, beautiful word. It carries both authority and specificity. It gives the sense that something important has been decided by someone who has every right to make that decision. In the world of work, being appointed to a new position was a big deal. It meant you were the one chosen for the task. It meant you were trusted.

You might have felt that when you retired, your appointments were over. You turned in the keys, signed the last form, and stepped out of the role that gave you a sense of being needed. But John 15:16 tells us that your most important appointment did not come from a human resources department or a board of directors. It came from Jesus.

Notice that the verse doesn't say you stumbled into your calling or just happened to be useful. You were chosen and appointed on purpose. And here is the best part: the fruit you bear was always meant to remain. In your career, much of what you produced was temporary. Emails were deleted, projects were finished, and budgets were reset every year. But the fruit of the Spirit—the love, joy, and peace you pour into others—is the kind of fruit that outlasts you. It keeps producing even after you are gone.

Our greatest influence often comes from staying connected to the Vine. You have been given a unique plot of land in God's Kingdom. Don't look over the fence at someone else's

field. Trust that the fruit growing in your life today is exactly what the world needs.

"The world tells us that if we aren't producing a paycheck, we aren't producing anything at all. It was hard at first to let go of performance-based thinking. But now, I am committed to praying as the most productive and lasting impact I can make." —
Doreen S.

This Week's Activity

Give something away this week. It doesn't have to involve money; best if it doesn't. It can be your time, your presence, your story, or your willingness to show up with a card on the doorstep of someone lonely. Give lavishly, with the full power of the Kingdom behind you.

Optional Radiance Journal Prompts

- When you think of the word appointed, how does it change how you feel about your daily schedule this week?
- Look at your ordinary life. Who are the people in your immediate circle who are hungry for the fruit of encouragement or hope?
- How does it feel to know that the work you do for the Kingdom today will remain long after your old work projects are forgotten?

Prayer

Lord, thank You for choosing me. It is hard to wrap my mind around the truth that You appointed me to bear fruit that

will last forever. Forgive me for thinking that my value ended when my job did. Please show me my appointed field this week. Open my eyes to the specific people and places where You want me to shine. Help me to give generously from the overflow of Your love. I want my life to produce a harvest that brings You glory. In Jesus' name, Amen.

> *"This is to My Father's glory, that you bear much fruit,*
> *proving yourselves to be My disciples." John 15:8*

Last week was about the appointment. This week is about the evidence.

Jesus doesn't say, "Bear some fruit." He says, "Bear much fruit." Not adequate fruit for someone your age. Not a reasonable harvest given your current season of life. Much. The word is deliberate, and it's not tied to your career status, your current energy levels, or how old you are. To the Father's glory, you were designed for abundance, and that design has not expired.

Jesus is not talking about productivity. He is talking about discipleship. The fruit He describes in John 15:8 is the visible evidence of a life lived close to Him. It is what people see in you and can't quite name. It is the way you stayed when it would have been easier to leave. The way you prayed for someone who never knew you were doing it. The way you showed up on a Tuesday with a casserole and no agenda. That is the "much" He is pointing to.

Think about the seeds you have already scattered that are still growing in other people's gardens. The encouragement you gave to your granddaughter the morning she almost quit. The conversation you had years ago with a young woman who was ready to walk away from her faith, and she didn't. The prayers you have whispered over the same person for fifteen years, even when nothing appeared to be changing. You may not see all of those plants from where

you are standing. But they are growing.

Nancy DeMoss Wolgemuth writes in *Choosing Gratitude* that one of the marks of a grateful life is the willingness to look for what God is doing in places you cannot see yet, trusting that faithfulness in ordinary moments produces fruit you cannot measure in ordinary ways. An ordinary morning spent in faithful prayer can shift the course of a family for generations. A small act of staying five minutes longer to listen, driving someone to a medical appointment, preparing a meal — none of these feel like much from the inside. But in the Father's hands, nothing offered in love is small.

The fruit that remains is not the fruit you planned out carefully or executed with strategy. It is the fruit that grows naturally from staying close to Him, from being the woman in the room who prays, who listens, who remembers, who tells the truth with kindness. That is the harvest Jesus is describing. And it is still being produced in your life today.

"I used to worry that retirement would leave me free, but still bored. Instead, I don't have time to be bored, because I finally have time to deepen relationships with people I truly love." — Tammy R.

Write your Fruit Inventory this week. Not a to-do list, but a look back. List the things you have poured yourself into that will live on after you: the testimony you shared, the person whose path changed because of a conversation with you, the prayers you have prayed for years, and the small kindnesses that felt ordinary when you offered them.

Optional Radiance Journal Prompts

- When you think about bearing much fruit, does it feel like a heavy assignment or a joyful overflow? What does your answer tell you about how you still see your own worth?
- Who is one person in your life today who is a direct recipient of fruit God has grown through you, perhaps without you ever realizing it?
- What is one small act of faithfulness from this past year that you have been tempted to dismiss as too small to matter?

Prayer

Lord, thank You that You measure my fruitfulness by my heart's connection to You, not by a title or a paycheck. Forgive me for the times I have looked at my ordinary days and thought the harvest was too small to count. Open my eyes to the much fruit You are already growing. Help me see the eternal weight in my prayers, my words, and my simple acts of love. Use this life to bring You great glory. In Jesus' name, Amen.

Week 48: Generous Sowing

Generosity in retirement looks different from what it did during your working years. Giving may have been tied to a financial transaction: writing a check, hitting a fundraising goal, or making sure the formal pledge was met. But now, the currency has shifted. Your most valuable assets aren't found in a ledger; they are found in your presence, your unhurried attention, and the deep well of stories you carry.

This week takes 2 Corinthians 9:6 beyond the financial and into the full range of what you have to give. To sow bountifully means giving your prayers, your focus, and your heart freely.

When you sow these seeds of presence, you are planting a harvest you cannot yet imagine. You might think a simple note or a long phone call is a small thing, but in the Kingdom of God, there is no such thing as a small seed. Every act of generosity performed in this new chapter of life can be used by our powerful God to grow into a legacy of faith that outlives you. You have been blessed with much, and now you have the beautiful opportunity to scatter that blessing everywhere you go.

"I have counted pennies all of my life out of fear of running out. Retirement is showing me that the things that truly hold value have nothing to do with money at all. And that realization allows me to give my time

more freely to people and causes that I really care about." — Beatrice K.

This Week's Activity

This week, we are returning to your gratitude lists from Week 19, but now we are going deeper. Gratitude grows with you, and what you see now, forty-eight weeks into this journey, will be much richer and more specific than what you saw the first time. Write a second round of thank-you notes. This time, focus on the people who specifically influenced your faith. Think of the Sunday school teacher from your childhood, the woman who prayed for you during a crisis, or the friend whose words of truth carried you through difficult years. Tell them exactly what their investment gave you. These notes take time to write well; this could become a weekly practice.

Optional Radiance Journal Prompts

- How has your definition of generosity changed since you left your full-time career?
- When you think about sowing bountifully, do you feel like you are giving from a place of scarcity or a place of overflow?
- Looking back at the people who influenced your faith, what was the seed they planted that has produced the most fruit in your life today?

Lord, thank You for the abundance You have poured into my life. Thank You that I have so much more than money to give. I want to be a woman who sows bountifully and joyfully. Please show me who needs my time, my stories, and my prayers this week. Help me to be a lavish giver of my presence. I trust You to take the seeds I plant and turn them into a harvest that brings You glory. In Jesus' name, Amen.

Week 49: A Good Person Leaves an Inheritance

When we hear the word inheritance, our minds often jump straight to bank accounts, property, or family heirlooms. We think about what we are leaving behind in a will. But the inheritance described in Proverbs 13:22 is about much more than money. It is everything that passes from one generation to the next through the intentional choices of someone who is thinking beyond her own lifetime.

For many of us, our careers were about building something for the present; meeting goals, earning a living, and providing for our needs. But now that the pace has slowed, you have the space to think about what you are building for the future. You are in a position to leave a wealth that cannot be taxed or spent. You are leaving a spiritual inheritance.

This week is a milestone. Everything we have walked through since Week 1 –discovering your identity, tracing God's faithfulness, and recognizing your crown of glory — has been leading to this moment. You are more than a woman who retired; you are a woman who has gathered a lifetime of truth, and that truth is a treasure for the people who come after you.

God uses our ordinary, everyday stories to reveal His extraordinary love. He reminds us that our lives are a living testimony. Your inheritance is the collection of God-

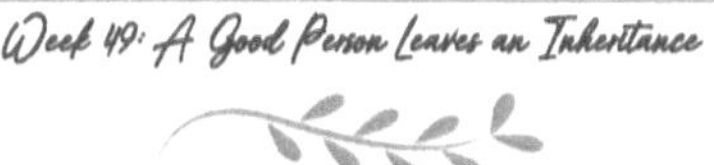

moments you have witnessed. It is the way you handled disappointment with grace. It is the way you prayed when there was no clear answer. It is the way you remained certain of God's goodness even when the world felt shaky.

> *"Don't let the enemy tell you that you don't have enough to give. Your family and your friends don't need a perfect grandmother or a perfect friend; they need someone who knows a perfect God. Telling them how He carried you is the best inheritance you could ever provide." — Joy T.*

Writing these things down is one of the most important things you will ever do. When you put your faith into words, you are building a bridge for your children and grandchildren to walk on. You are giving them a map for their own hard days. This isn't about being perfect; it's about being real. They don't need to hear that you never struggled because you walked with God; they need to hear how God met you in the struggle.

Write your Legacy Letter this week. Address it to the people you love most. Tell them what you know about God that took you a lifetime to learn. Tell them what you see in them that they don't yet see in themselves. Tell them the truth about the hard chapters of your life and what those times actually gave you. Tell them what you have been praying for them, specifically and faithfully, across the years. Write it the way you would speak if you knew it was your last chance to say every important thing. Then seal it and put it somewhere safe where they will find it. This letter is worth more than anything in a bank account.

- If you could only pass on one single truth about God to the next generation, what would it be?
- When you think about the people you love, what inheritance of character or faith do you see already growing in them?
- What is a story of God's rescue in your life that you haven't shared with your family yet?
- How does it feel to realize that your most valuable work is being done with a pen and a heart full of love rather than a professional title?

Prayer

Lord, thank You for the wealth of wisdom and faith You have allowed me to gather over the years. Thank You for the treasure to leave behind that is eternal. Please give me the right words as I write this letter. Help me to speak from a place of joy and clarity. I pray that my words will be a light for my family for years to come. May they see Your faithfulness through my story and put their trust in You. In Jesus' name, Amen.

Week 50: Iron Sharpens Iron

> *"As iron sharpens iron, so one man sharpens another."*
> Proverbs 27:17

Think back to those first few days after you turned in your keys and your laptop. There was probably a bit of static in the air; a mix of excitement and a nagging question about who you were going to be without a commute. But over the last fifty weeks, the static has started to clear.

Proverbs 27:17 is a beautiful image of mutual formation. In the ancient world, a dull blade was useless until it met the friction of another piece of metal. It took heat, pressure, and contact to bring out the edge. Our friendships in Christ work the same way. We don't grow in a vacuum; we grow because of the sisters who love us enough to tell us the truth, pray us through the hard Tuesdays, and remind us of who we are when we forget.

Retirement gives you a unique advantage in this sharpening process. For years, your social interactions might have been dictated by the office hierarchy or the speed of the school run. Now, your connections can be driven by intentionality. You have the time to be the iron for someone else.

> *"I spent my career trying to 'climb' past other people. Now that I'm choosing to walk with women, there is nothing quite like this new sisterhood of helping each other grow into their God-given purposes." —*
> *Marilyn H.*

This Week's Activity

Write a thank-you note to the person who has sharpened you most this year. This is different from a general thank-you; it is specifically about who you are *becoming* because of their influence. Tell them exactly what has changed in your heart because of their friendship. Then, identify one woman you can begin investing in more intentionally. You don't need a formal mentoring title. Just look for someone who needs a sister to point out the gold in her life. Go first. Reach out and start the conversation.

- See if you can name at least three women in your sharpening circle who have kept your faith strong and bright over your lifetime.
- When was a time this year when a friend's friction — a challenging piece of advice —may have stung but made you a better version of yourself?

Lord, thank You for the gift of sisterhood in Christ. Thank You for the women who have loved me enough to sharpen me, even when it felt like friction. Forgive me for the times I've tried to grow on my own. Please show me the woman who needs Your strength this week. Give me the words to encourage her and the eyes to see her the way You do. Help my friendships to be a place where we both become more like Jesus every day. In Jesus' name, Amen.

Week 51: I Have Finished the Race

> *"I have fought the good fight, I have finished the race, I have kept the faith." 2 Timothy 4:7*

We stand at the penultimate week of our year together. When Paul wrote these words, he was not sitting in a comfortable retirement villa with a view of the Mediterranean (though perhaps you are!). He was writing from a cold prison cell, aware that his earthly life was nearing its end. Yet he described his life with remarkable completeness. He had fought the fight. He had run the race. He had kept the faith. For Paul, finishing well was more than comfort and glory.

In Week 47, we took an inventory of the fruit that remains in your life. This week is different. Fruit reflects what God has produced through your life for others. You might have thought that when you retired, the race was over. You might have felt like you stepped off the track and into the bleachers. But the Bible doesn't describe our later years as a seat in the stands. It describes them as a continuation of the course God set for us before we were even born.

You have fought a good fight. You fought for your family, you fought for your integrity in the workplace, and you fought to keep your joy when life was heavy. You have finished many courses—graduation, career milestones, raising children—and now you are running this new, unhurried course with a different kind of grace. Most importantly, you have kept the faith. Through the decades of Monday mornings and Friday deadlines, you didn't let go of the One who was holding you.

You are not finished yet. The finish line for a believer isn't a retirement party; it is the moment we see His face. Until then, we keep running. The evidence of your endurance is on every page of this devotional you have completed. You are a finisher. You are a woman who stays the course. Take a look at how far you have come and let it give you the momentum to keep going.

> *"Finishing well doesn't mean having it all figured out; it just means not giving up. I've had some stumbles and some slow miles lately, but as long as I'm moving toward Him, I'm running a winning race. My faith is the only trophy I really care about keeping." — Patty G.*

This Week's Activity

Is there something you've been putting off that needs to be done? This week, do it. We aren't talking about an enormous project that requires months of work, but that specific thing that keeps showing up on your mental to-do list and keeps getting moved to later.

The accumulation of small completions builds a momentum that carries you further. The woman who finishes what she starts learns to trust herself more, and that trust is a powerful tool for the days ahead. Do the thing you keep avoiding. Finish it on purpose.

Optional Radiance Journal Prompts

- When you look back at the fight of your career years, what is the one victory of character you are most proud of today?

- Paul mentions keeping the faith. What is one specific time this year when your faith felt tested, but you chose to hold on anyway?
- How does it feel to realize that your race didn't end when you stopped receiving a paycheck?
- What is one mile of your current life—perhaps a new hobby, a relationship, or a ministry—that you want to run with more intentional joy this year?

Prayer

Lord, thank You for the strength You have given me to run this far. I praise You that You have been my coach, my water, and my strength in every mile. Forgive me for the times I've wanted to quit or felt like I was finished before You said I was. Thank You for the gift of this new course. Help me to fight the good fight of faith today and to finish my small tasks with excellence. I want to be a woman who keeps the faith until the very end. In Jesus' name, Amen.

"In old age they will still bear fruit; healthy and green they will remain." Psalm 92:14

We have come full circle. We are back at the very verse that launched your journey with this book. When you first read these words in Week 1, they might have felt like a lovely wish or a poetic idea. But today, after fifty-two weeks (or longer) of walking this path, you aren't just reading this verse; I hope you are living it. You have the sap of God's daily renewal in your veins and the green of new growth in your spirit.

This year has been a journey of discovery. You have moved through four distinct phases: You have Awakened to your true identity. You've learned to Flourish in the quiet, been Strengthened for a new kind of courage, and discovered just how fruitful your life remains. You have traced the All-Along thread of your story and realized that God never missed a single stitch. You have written your Legacy Letter and your lasting Fruit Inventory. You have learned that receiving grace is just as important as giving it, and you have discovered that God's morning mercies are as fresh and dependable as the dew.

You walked out of your workplace for the last time, perhaps feeling a bit uncertain about the words for your new life. Now, you have them. You are God's handiwork. You are a crown of glory. You are an appointed fruit-bearer. You are flourishing.

"For most of my life, I thought my best years were the ones I could prove with a resume, but this year has shown me that my best years are the ones I'm proving with my peace. I feel more alive than I was at twenty-five because I finally know who I am apart from what I do." — Eleanor W.

This Week's Activity

Pull out your copy of the Flourish Journey Map, and write your Flourishing Manifesto today. Use one full page, your own words, and your own voice. Start it with this sentence: I am God's handiwork. From there, write out what you now know to be true about your identity, your purpose, and your future. Write about the faithfulness you've seen and the fruit you look forward to bearing. End it, however, in a way that feels most true to your heart. Sign it and date it. This isn't just a piece of paper; it is the charter for the rest of your life.

Optional Radiance Journal Prompts

- Look back at the woman who started Week 1. What is the biggest change you see?
- Which of the four phases (Awaken, Flourish, Strengthen, Fruitful) felt like the most important breakthrough for you personally?
- How does the image of being full of sap and green change the way you look at your physical health and your mental energy this week?
- What is one bold prayer you are carrying into next year, knowing now that God answers better than you dare to ask?

Lord, I stand before You today with a heart full of gratitude. Thank You for leading me through this year and for showing me that my life has no expiration date in Your Kingdom. Thank You for Your Spirit that keeps me fresh and the green of Your grace that keeps me growing. I choose to live out my manifesto every single day. Help me to stay rooted in Your love and to keep bearing fruit that brings You glory. I am Your handiwork, and I am so excited for the life we are building together. In Jesus' name, Amen.

Anchoring verses that establish the book's core theology.

Identity/Purpose: "For we are God's workmanship, created in Christ Jesus to do good works, which God prepared in advance as our way of life." Ephesians 2:10

The "Flourishing" Verse (Vitality/Growth): "The righteous will flourish like a palm tree, and grow like a cedar in Lebanon. Planted in the house of the LORD, they will flourish in the courts of our God. In old age they will still bear fruit; healthy and green they will remain." Psalm 92:12–14

The "Reveal" Verse (Light/Direction): "The path of the righteous is like the first gleam of dawn, shining brighter and brighter until midday." Proverbs 4:18

Verses for stillness, fresh starts, and God's gentle, daily replenishment.

"Because of the loving devotion of the LORD we are not consumed, for His mercies never fail. They are new every morning; great is Your faithfulness!" Lamentations 3:22–23

"I will be like the dew to Israel; he will blossom like the lily and take root like the cedars of Lebanon." Hosea 14:5

"From the womb of the dawn, to you belongs the dew of your youth." Psalm 110:3

"Therefore we do not lose heart. Though our outer self is wasting away, yet our inner self is being renewed day by

day." 2 Corinthians 4:16

"Be still and know that I am God;" Psalm 46:10

"I ask that the eyes of your heart may be enlightened, so that you may know the hope of His calling, the riches of His glorious inheritance in the saints." Ephesians 1:18

Verses affirming that God's lifelong design is intentional and unbroken.

"Your eyes saw my unformed body; all my days were written in Your book and ordained for me before one of them came to be." Psalm 139:16

"Before I formed you in the womb I knew you, and before you were born I set you apart." Jeremiah 1:5

"Do not fear, for I have redeemed you; I have called you by your name; you are Mine!" Isaiah 43:1

Verses That Honestly Address the Aging Body While Promising Sustained Spiritual Vigor.

"Even to your old age, I will be the same, and I will bear you up when you turn gray. I have made you and I will carry you; I will sustain you and deliver you." Isaiah 46:4

"Gray hair is a crown of glory; it is attained along the path of righteousness." Proverbs 16:31

"Who satisfies you with good things, so that your youth is renewed like the eagle's." Psalm 103:5

"But those who wait upon the LORD will renew their strength; they will mount up with wings like eagles; they will run and not grow weary, they will walk and not faint." Isaiah 40:31

Identity: Verses for Anchoring in Christ

"I praise You, for I am fearfully and wonderfully made. Marvelous are Your works, and I know this very well." Psalm 139:14

"For you died, and your life is now hidden with Christ in God." Colossians 3:3

"I have been crucified with Christ, and I no longer live, but Christ lives in me." Galatians 2:20

Verses focusing on visibility, warmth, and the inner light that comes from God

"Those who look to Him are radiant with joy; their faces shall never be ashamed." Psalm 34:5

"Arise, shine, for your light has come, and the glory of the LORD rises upon you." Isaiah 60:1

"In the same way, let your light shine before men, that they may see your good deeds and glorify your Father in heaven." Matthew 5:16

Verses for confidence, boundary-setting, stepping out, and fearless living.

"The wicked flee when no one pursues, but the righteous are

as bold as a lion." Proverbs 28:1

"No, in all these things we are more than conquerors through Him who loved us." Romans 8:37

"For God has not given us a spirit of fear, but of power, love, and self-control." 2 Timothy 1:7

Verses for looking back at God's faithfulness and passing the baton forward.

"For I know the plans I have for you, declares the LORD, plans to prosper you and not to harm you, to give you a future and a hope." Jeremiah 29:11

"I have fought the good fight, I have finished the race, I have kept the faith." 2 Timothy 4:7

The "Go Deeper" List

A curated collection of books for when your heart wants a little more.

Gratitude & Spiritual Formation

Wolgemuth, Nancy DeMoss. *Choosing Gratitude: Your Journey to Joy*. Chicago: Moody Publishers, 2009. The gold standard. If you want to learn how to actually live a life of thankfulness (even when things are messy), start here.

Murray, Andrew. *Abide in Christ*. A total classic, published in 1864, for when you're tired of "doing" and just want to practice "being" with Jesus. It's like a deep breath for your soul.

Cowman, L. B. E., and Jim Reimann. *Streams in the Desert*. Grand Rapids: Zondervan, 1997. There's a reason women have kept this on their nightstands for a century—it is pure comfort for those seasons where life feels a bit dry.

DeMoss, Nancy Leigh. *Holiness: The Heart God Purifies*. Chicago: Moody Publishers, 2004

Edwards, Jonathan. *The End for Which God Created the World*. Published in 1765

Prayer & Breath

Tucker, Jennifer. *Breath as Prayer*. Thomas Nelson, 2022.

Lewis, C. S. *How to Pray: Reflections and Essays*. Harper Collins, 2020. It's C. S. Lewis, so you know it's brilliant. He has a way of making the "mystery" of prayer feel

approachable and natural.

Murray, Andrew. *Lord, Teach Us to Pray*. Published in 1896. If you've ever felt like you "don't know how to pray," Andrew Murray is the gentle teacher you've been looking for.

Graham, Billy. *The Holy Spirit: Activating God's Power in Your Life*. Nashville: Thomas Nelson, 1988. We often forget we don't have to do life in our own strength. This book is a great reminder of how the Holy Spirit actually helps us day-to-day.

Kendall, R. T. *40 Days With the Holy Spirit*. Lake Mary, FL: Charisma House, 2014. I love this one because it's a journey. It's perfect if you want to get to know the Holy Spirit as a person and a friend, not just a concept.

Jeremiah, David. *When Your World Falls Apart*. Dallas: Word Publishing, 2004. For the days when life feels like it's crumbling. It's incredibly kind and practical, and it helps you see a way forward when you feel stuck in the pain.

Caine, Christine. *The Faith to Flourish: God's Design for a Rooted, Resilient, and Fruitful Life*. Nashville: Nelson Books, 2026

ten Boom, Corrie, with John and Elizabeth Sherrill. *The Hiding Place*. New York: Bantam Books, 1971

Kendall, R. T. *Total Forgiveness*. Lake Mary, FL: Charisma House, 2001

Sande, Ken. *The Peacemaker: A Biblical Guide to Resolving Personal Conflict*. Grand Rapids: Baker Books, 1991

Lewis, C. S. *The Weight of Glory*. New York: Macmillan, 1949. (Originally delivered as a sermon in 1941)

Mind, Body, and Rest

Allen, Jennie. *Get Out of Your Head: Stopping the Spiral of Toxic Thoughts*. Colorado Springs: WaterBrook, 2020

Amen M.D., Daniel G. *Change Your Brain Every Day: Simple Daily Practices to Strengthen Your Mind, Memory, Moods, Energy, Habits, and Relationships*. Carol Stream: Tyndale Refresh, 2023

Dalton-Smith, Saundra. *Sacred Rest: Recover Your Life, Renew Your Energy, Restore Your Sanity*. New York: FaithWords, 2017

Walker, Matthew. *Why We Sleep: Unlocking the Power of Sleep and Dreams*. New York: Scribner, 2017

Cited Studies & Research

Emmons, Robert A., and Michael E. McCullough. "Counting Blessings Versus Burdens: An Experimental Investigation of Gratitude and Subjective Well-Being in Daily Life." Journal of Personality and Social Psychology 84, no. 2 (2003): 377–389

Research & Sources

Wilson, R. S., et al. "Cognitive Activity and the Cognitive Morbidity of Alzheimer Disease." *Neurology*, 2013

Van der Weel, F. R., and A. L. H. Van der Meer. "Handwriting, Not Typewriting, Leads to Widespread Brain Connectivity." *Frontiers in Psychology*, 2023

Let Others Know What You Thought!

If there is someone you know could benefit from this book, and if you haven't done so yet, consider leaving an honest review. Reviews help others discover books like this. You can scan the QR code here: